What People Are Saying About James W. Goll and *The Feeler*...

My dear friend James Goll is a disciplined student of the Word and a prolific writer. He lives to communicate the heart of God for our lives. His latest book, *The Feeler: Discovering How Sensitivity Helps You Discern and Act on God's Voice*, is timely and greatly needed. And as far as I know, it is the only book of its kind. The sensitivities of our lives are typically shut down in favor of the intellect. Many people don't realize that God doesn't always speak to the mind first. Even the brilliant apostle Paul taught that the kingdom of God is *righteousness, peace, and joy*, which means two-thirds of the kingdom are *felt* realities. In *The Feeler*, you will see and hear the insights of someone who has successfully navigated the one part of the Christian life that most leaders would like to avoid. I believe this book will have a powerful impact on all who read it.

—*Bill Johnson*
Author, *Born for Significance* and *The Way of Life*
Bethel Church, Redding, CA

James Goll is one of the most accurate prophets I know. For years, Christians have tried to shut down their emotions. James's breakthrough book *The Feeler* will stop you from ignoring this God-given aspect of your life and enable you to discern the gift of the prophetic voice in your emotions.

—*Sid Roth*
Host, *It's Supernatural!*

A dear friend for decades, James Goll has proven to be a unique gift to the church and to me personally, excelling in his God-ordained roles as a seasoned prophet, teacher, and writer. His newest book, *The Feeler*, shares his down-to-earth perspective on the role of emotions in the life of a spiritually mature believer. I believe you will be equipped and inspired by powerful insights into the Word of God as you embark on this eye-opening journey in the spirit. More than just a book, *The Feeler* is an invitation to encounter God in fresh ways, to be activated in your Spirit-empowered senses, and to walk more fully into your divine calling!

—*Dr. Ché Ahn*
Founder and President, Harvest International Ministry
Founding and Senior Pastor, Harvest Rock Church, Pasadena, CA
International Chancellor, Wagner University
Ché Ahn Ministries

James Goll shares my vision to bring the supernatural power of God to this generation, and he has a distinct calling in this realm. God gives us signs and wonders not for their own sake but so they will lead us to have a deep relationship with the living God. In his new book, *The Feeler*, James combines what he has learned in decades of ministry to show you how to hear God's voice, discern spiritual atmospheres, demolish the plans of the enemy, and be so attuned to the works of the Father that you walk in step with His Spirit every moment of the day. Through this book, you will learn to receive the fullness of God's life and be prepared to reach out to others with His powerful peace, healing, and deliverance!

—*Apostle Guillermo Maldonado*
Founder, King Jesus International Ministry, Miami, FL
Best-selling author of many books, including *Jesus Is Coming Soon*, *Breakthrough Prayer*, and *How to Walk in the Supernatural Power of God*

God wants to open the glories of His heavens to us, touching our lives and the lives of people around us with discernment, healing, divine intervention, deliverance, and much more. And He has provided various power portals for us to receive His heavenly gifts. Some of these portals are in our own bodies but need to be spiritually activated. In *The Feeler*, James Goll vividly explains how our physical senses can be gateways into the supernatural realm and that we should invite the Holy Spirit to help us make the appropriate connections. Through this book, you will expand the breadth and depth of your understanding and practice of living in the Spirit. Release your senses and emotions to God and allow Him to speak to you, to demonstrate His love in myriad ways, and to bring His glory realms to earth.

—*Joshua Mills*
Recording artist, keynote conference speaker, and author of more than twenty books, including *Power Portals, Moving in Glory Realms,* and *7 Divine Mysteries*
www.joshuamills.com

The Feeler is an excellent work by James W. Goll that aptly teaches how to be a God-centered, spiritual person in a material world. This book focuses rightly on the process of spiritual growth as a function of training our natural senses to interact with the spiritual realm all the time. We cannot lean on our own understanding and walk with God at the same time. The power of life in the Spirit is activated by our own decisions to humbly rely on His supernatural grace and insights, rather than our own opinions and thinking. James Goll has provided us with clear guidelines so that we can live the life of Christ as He did on this earth.

—*Joan Hunter*
Author and evangelist

Many people are earnestly seeking transformation in their lives, their families, their work, or their ministry. If you want to experience such change, so much depends on your hearing God's voice, understanding His will, and walking in His power. You need to know all the means God has given you for connecting with Him and flowing in His Spirit. With James Goll's new book, *The Feeler*, you will learn the dynamic connection between your senses—both physical and spiritual—and discerning what God wants to say to you and receiving what He wants to give you. Among other insights, James shares how to integrate your senses with the exercise of your spiritual gifts and the development of the fruit of the Spirit in your life. Discover how this unique "Feeler realm" can come alive for you as you yield to God and allow Him to empower you in breakthrough for "a new day and a new era"!

—*Matt Sorger*
Prophetic healing revivalist
Author, *God's Unstoppable Breakthrough*
Founder, Glory Life echurch
mattsorger.com

James Goll is a powerful prophet, an anointed teacher, a gifted story-teller, and an insightful author on so many prophetic subjects. His latest book, *The Feeler: Discovering How Sensitivity Helps You Discern and Act on God's Voice*, equips believers to understand the role our emotions and five natural senses play in hearing the voice of God and discerning His heart. This book explodes with wisdom and fresh insight that will cause God's supernatural realm to become more tangible in the reader's life. Prepare to be strengthened and challenged in your walk with God as "the Feeler realm" is opened to you in a new way.

—*Jane Hamon*
Vision Church @ Christian International
Prophet, teacher, and author, *Dreams and Visions, The Deborah Company, The Cyrus Decree, Discernment,* and *Declarations for Breakthrough*

Many believers experience feelings and senses that perplex them. They wonder, "Where is this coming from? Is this me? What do I do with this?" In James Goll's book *The Feeler: Discovering How Sensitivity Helps You Discern and Act on God's Voice*, you will learn how to discern those feelings and senses and how to grow in sensitivity to the nudges of the Spirit of God. There is very little teaching available in the church on this subject. I'm thrilled that James has produced this wonderful resource. He is always Scripture-based, seasoned in Holy Spirit-directed encounters, and full of wisdom in delivery and implementation. You will discover many valuable keys in this book that will grant you much-desired understanding.

—*Patricia King*
Minister, author, and television host

James Goll is such an immense treasure trove of wisdom, knowledge, and revelation on anything and everything to do with spiritual sensing and discerning. No matter what level of discernment you presently have, this forerunner book on the Feeler realm will provide you with an on-ramp to go to the next level. The chapters on refining your spiritual senses and on sensitivity are indeed priceless. For James and other disciples of Jesus like him, it is all connected to growing in greater intimacy with God—and that will be the lasting, supernatural fruit of your reading this wonderful book.

—*Johnny Enlow*
International speaker and author, *The Seven Mountain Mandate*

James Goll is not just a dear friend; I consider him to be one of profound mind and insight in relation to prophetic perception. As the church continues to move forward into the intention of God for its future, more and more you will be hearing of the need for a Pentecostal and charismatic "Theology of Discernment." As people who believe in the fullness of the Spirit, our comprehension of the process of perception and discernment is influenced by our encounters with God the Father's threefold cord, which is never to be separated: the Holy Spirit, the Son of God, and the Scriptures. We, as God's company of prophetic and kingly priests, are coming to terms with how to enter into the purposes of God with discernment that brings about His desired results. James's newest release, *The Feeler*, is a perfect follow-up to his classic work *The Discerner*. *The Feeler* gives us all a seat at the table where this conversation is taking place—and will continue to take place and expand as we move forward into the future Jesus has prepared for us. My thanks to James for taking on this topic. As you read, you will discover how James's brilliance shines on every page!

—*Dr. Mark J. Chironna*
Church On The Living Edge
Mark Chironna Ministries, Longwood, FL

As believers, all of us have the ability to hear God's voice, although how we *primarily* hear from Him or obtain revelation may be different from the next person. Many of us are wired to first discern through our feelings what God is doing, then knowing or supernaturally seeing follows. James Goll's newest book, *The Feeler*, is being released at this pivotal moment in history to instruct us how to discern, in the "Feeler realm," what God is saying. It's an encouragement that our feelings often lead to the discovery of the "more" that God has for us in the supernatural. Be encouraged! You are hearing from God through what you are sensing and feeling!

—*Ana Werner*
Founder, Ana Werner Ministries
President, Eagles Network
Author, *The Seer's Path*, *Seeing Behind the Veil*, and *The Warrior's Dance*

Devour this book. James Goll gives us not just an understanding of the theology of discernment in how to better hear God's voice, but also in how these principles apply to our daily lives. Through many years of experience and ministry, James is able to impart truths in practical ways to others. I encourage every believer who desires to grow in the areas of discernment and the prophetic to study *The Feeler.*

—*Dr. Mahesh Chavda*
All Nations Church, Charlotte, NC

One of my deep concerns for the church is that many believers haven't been equipped to walk in the supernatural power that God has made available to them, and therefore they remain discouraged and defeated in their lives. We need more teaching about how God is continually reaching out to help us and wants us to live in peace, strength, and victory in our Christian lives. James Goll is a gifted teacher with a pastor's heart who shares a groundbreaking message for the body of Christ. In his new book *The Feeler,* he explains how God has specifically designed us to hear Him and to serve Him with not only our spirits, minds, and wills but also our emotions. When we learn to employ the full range of our God-given senses, we will be supernaturally equipped in new and powerful ways to receive from Him in the heavenly realms and then to reach out to other people with His love, grace, healing, freedom, purpose, and victory.

—*Dr. Kynan T. Bridges*
Pastor, Grace & Peace Global Fellowship
Author, *Unlocking the Code of the Supernatural, School of the Miraculous,*
and *The Power of Prophetic Prayer*

James Goll's book *The Feeler* explores a dimension that at times has been greatly overlooked, especially if we are not tuned in to the nuances of the Holy Spirit's directives. As you read this book, you will be awakened into a whole new realm of insight, guidance, and revelation. You will be invited into another class in the School of the Holy Spirit of Hearing and Obeying the Voice of God. James is pioneering for the body of Christ once again, as he did previously with his classic books *The Seer* and *The Discerner*. Add *The Feeler* to your arsenal, and you will be more equipped and ready than ever before!

—*Steven and Renee Springer*
Cofounders, Global Presence Ministries

THE

Feeler

THE

Feeler

DISCOVERING HOW SENSITIVITY HELPS YOU
DISCERN AND ACT ON GOD'S VOICE

JAMES W. GOLL

AUTHOR OF NATIONAL BEST SELLER *THE SEER*

WHITAKER
HOUSE

THE FEELER:
Discovering How Sensitivity Helps You Discern and Act on God's Voice

James W. Goll
God Encounters Ministries
P.O. Box 1653 ◆ Franklin, TN 37065
www.godencounters.com ◆ www.GOLLIdeation.com
info@godencounters.com

ISBN: 978-1-64123-582-2 ◆ eBook ISBN: 978-1-64123-583-9
Printed in the United States of America
© 2021 by James W. Goll

Whitaker House
1030 Hunt Valley Circle ◆ New Kensington, PA 15068
www.whitakerhouse.com

LC record available at https://lccn.loc.gov/2020051298
LC ebook record available at https://lccn.loc.gov/2020051299

1 2 3 4 5 6 7 8 9 10 11 ⟪⟫ 28 27 26 25 24 23 22 21

Dedication

I dedicate this book to my Assistant and Helper for many years, the Holy Spirit. You are my constant Companion, Tutor, and Guide. You bring forth gifts and fruit that are equally supernatural into and through my life. Over the years, I have learned that what is important for spiritual discernment is not only the sensitivity of the believer, but also our learning and acknowledging the nature of the Holy Spirit Himself. I am so grateful for the third person of the Blessed Trinity—the Holy Spirit. Therefore, it is my joy to dedicate this book, *The Feeler*, to the Holy Spirit.

Acknowledgment

While it is always a team effort to bring forth a major project such as this, there are often key players. Some are assigned to work with you on one project and one alone. Then there are others. Kathy Deering fits into a category all her own. This dear woman of God has been my writing assistant for well over a decade. She has taken my rough drafts, smoothed them out, and filled in many gaps. She has corrected my grammatical glitches and reordered my scattered thoughts into a more cohesive work.

This is our last project to work on together as she now retires from her full-time vocation of writing, editing, and assisting others with their manuscripts. So, with a heart full of gratitude, I wish to acknowledge only one person—Kathy Deering. Her expertise has been heard and felt on every page of my many manuscripts that have reached across the globe.

Thank you, Kathy, for your dedication to the Lord Jesus Christ and for being such a dependable person of excellence. Blessings to you and your family in the next phase of your life and ministry.

Contents

Foreword

I am so glad that you are choosing to read James Goll's newest book, *The Feeler*. This is a historic book and, to my knowledge, a first of its kind.

My husband, Mike, and I have known James for many years. We have prayed together, laughed together, shared meals together, and wept over serious situations together—and I can tell you that what he has written is authentic. Because of our natural and spiritual affinity, James and I often chuckle and say, "We are really more like brother and sister than friends!"

One personal anecdote: At the first prophetic gathering of what is now the Apostolic Council of Prophetic Elders, more than twenty years ago, a spirit of travail hit me, and I started weeping over America. This was before 9/11, and we had received a serious word of warning for the US about something of gigantic and tragic proportions that was headed toward the nation.

Falling on my knees, I wept and wept. As I quieted my weeping, I heard another sound of loud sobbing to my left. I turned to see James Goll on his knees, with racking cries coming out of his mouth. That is how I really came to know him. Bonded in friendship through crisis intercession.

Many leaders, even Christian leaders, are afraid of being vulnerable. They might feel that they will be seen as "lesser" in the eyes of the people who listen to them for guidance. James is not one of them. I guess once you have stared down death four times in your life, you get a different perspective on what's important. James writes from a place of having lived through the refiner's fire on a level that I have never personally experienced.

These circumstances, and more—such as the loss of his wife, my dear, dear friend Michal Ann, whose stories he weaves throughout these pages—have refined him. He writes as a survivor and with the heart of a lover of Jesus in spite of all he has gone through.

As you read some of his personal story, you will realize that, in the natural, James had only a slim chance of ever rising to become the world-renowned prophetic voice that he is today. I appreciate his transparency and willingness to be a risk-taker as he shares his journey, including his struggles.

I love the preface to *The Feeler*! James writes about how he could have been a person who saw his "extra-sensitive" nature as a curse, but he came to understand that it was a gift and blessing from God. This realization has prompted him to share what he has learned as tools to help other believers in their spiritual understanding and growth.

The first chapter of the book is entitled "Experiencing the Emotions of God." As James so aptly teaches us, God has emotions! He laughs, He cries, He mourns, and He rejoices! Since we are made in His image, and His emotions are, we could say, supernatural, it stands to reason that we need to recognize our own emotions and navigate them in a way that brings blessings, both personal and corporate.

James jumps right in and shows us that God takes delight in His people. I love that God takes delight in me! It brings tears to my eyes just to think of it. As Christians, we talk and sing about the love of the Father, but sometimes I pause and ask myself, "Do I realize what a gift that is?" Through the years, I have often joked, "I am God's favorite! Of course, you may think that you are, but I really know that I am!" In truth, God is loving and big enough that, in the most supernatural way, each one of us is His favorite!

One of the statements in *The Feeler* that I found to be especially powerful is this one: "An emotion, after all, happens to be a lively and vigorous activity of the mind, not a separate function outside the operation of the mind." We must learn how our emotions contribute to the way our soul functions. And as James says, "Our spirit, soul, and body work together at all times. It takes all three components, united and functioning as one, to represent the image of the triune God."

Every believer would do well not only to enjoy this book, but also to study it. A few times, I laughed out loud while reading it! Whether or not you are a born Feeler, you probably have one in your family. You may even be married to one. You need this book! And, if you operate in the prophetic realm and/or teach on it, *The Feeler* is an excellent resource for your own spiritual life and for effective mentoring.

Get ready to open yourself up to a whole new, wonderful world of feeling God's presence, hearing His voice, and using all of the senses He has given you to serve Him and His people.

God bless you!

—*Cindy Jacobs*
Dallas, TX

Preface:
Once More, with Feeling

I'm a "feeler," a touchy-feely kind of a guy who can wear my emotions on my sleeve, as some say. It has been quite a journey learning how to navigate this dimension of being extra-sensitive and eventually learn to see this quality as a blessing and not a curse. What a roller-coaster ride it has been to learn how to redemptively yield this realm to the Holy Spirit and not let it control me. Yes, my senses and feelings play a very big part in how I interact with people—and with God.

Being a Feeler has forced me to be a ponderer when it comes to figuring out how a person like me clicks, let alone fits into the body of Christ. In all of my teachings, I emphasize the idea of laying a firm foundation for faith and life; and in my case, that includes a dogged pursuit to understand what I have come to call the "Feeler realm."

For the longest time, I had more questions than answers. I wondered: How does my emotional side fit with God's truth? As a "mature believer," am I not expected to be sober-minded, circumspect, and slow to anger? Are negative emotions such as fear just plain wrong? Am I supposed to rebuke my passions, die to them, or what? How do joyful and exciting emotions fit into my godly lifestyle? What's the proper balance between intellect and emotion? Many of you may know of my efforts to find a balance between the right (creative) and the left (logical) brain functions!

I also wondered why human emotions seem to get such a bad rap in the church. What does God's Word say about emotions, and how should I understand what I read there? What is the ideal way to handle my personal emotions? Should I consider them good, bad, or neutral? How should emotions look in the life of a mature believer? How does the emotional side of someone's personality blend with spiritual gifts? Should I consider my emotions to be a help or a hindrance when it comes to serving in God's kingdom?

Every question raises new ones. Where do all those emotional feelings come from, anyway? Do they reflect the qualities of the Creator in whose image we have been created? In other words, do we worship an emotional Godhead? Or is He objective and far removed from the messy business of human interactions? Can we ever know how God feels—assuming He even has emotions?

During my ponderings over the years, I knew that Jesus showed anger when He drove the moneychangers out of the temple (see, for example, Matthew 21:12–13) and that He also showed compassion and sympathy: *"Jesus wept"* (John 11:35). But isn't that only because the Son of God was also a man, which puts Him in a different category from the other two persons of the Trinity?

And...are these even the right questions to ask?

One day, I stumbled onto this passage from the prophet Isaiah, and I was surprised and reassured to see such a variety of strong emotions pouring out of the heart of the Lord God:

> I [the LORD God] *was amazed to see that no one intervened to help the oppressed. So I myself stepped in to save them with my strong arm, and my wrath sustained me.... I will tell of the LORD's unfailing love. I will praise the LORD for all he has done. I will rejoice in his great goodness to Israel, which he has granted according to his*

mercy and love. He said, "They are my very own people. Surely they will not betray me again." And he became their Savior. In all their suffering he also suffered, and he personally rescued them. In his love and mercy he redeemed them. He lifted them up and carried them through all the years.   (Isaiah 63:5, 7–9 NLT)

These verses of Scripture confirmed what I knew was true—our human emotions reflect the emotional aspects of the Creator God who has made us in His own image. Therefore, emotions must have a vital place in any believer's life—not just in the lives of us so-called Feelers. The fact is, all God's creatures have a place in the choir, whether they start out singing with "feeling" or not. So, even if you don't consider yourself to be an "emotional" person, I encourage you to keep reading and learn what God's Word has to say on this subject. Discover how sanctified feelings and emotions can deepen your walk with the Lord, enabling you to love and serve Him more fully.

I completely understand that we are supposed to walk by faith and not by sight or by our feelings and emotions. In this book, I don't suggest that we are to just ride the wave of doing what feels good in any given moment. I also don't think we should be "moody blues" believers.

In the following chapters, I cover many aspects of this somewhat slippery and sometimes complex subject of emotions and feelings. I present new concepts and might even introduce some new terminology, providing ways for believers to live comfortably amid the freedoms and boundaries of these everyday pulls and pushes within ourselves and with others.

I'm not a licensed psychologist, but I do have a degree in basic social work that I earned many years ago. I also don't have a professional seminary degree in biblical studies, so I can't claim on that basis to have the last word on multiple things of God. Yet I do bring to the plate an integrated approach to life and ministry, with years of experience, a doctorate in practical ministry, a certification as a Life Language Coach, a role of adviser to inner healing and counseling ministries, and experience as a consultant for leaders in both the business and church spheres.

I have devoted much effort to develop a thorough study of how our human emotions help us discern the will of God and act accordingly. It is my great and sincere desire to help people serve the King and His kingdom more freely, not only with their minds but also through their hearts.

Over the years, I felt like a pioneer in new territory, "feeling" my way up various emotional mountains of joy and accomplishment as well as through valleys of disappointment and heartache. Now, I invite you to accompany me on this continuing journey, which is full of excitement and anticipation for what is around the next bend in the road. Let's launch out, redeeming a new realm—the Feeler realm—in Jesus's name!

1

Experiencing the Emotions of God

"These things I have spoken to you, that My joy may remain in you, and that your joy may be full."
—John 15:11 (NKJV)

Let's go for the jugular right at the beginning! Does God have emotions? Some theologians say no; they declare that an all-powerful, supreme God must be "impassible," that He doesn't have passions, as we do. And if He does, He doesn't exhibit them openly, as we do. After a lifetime of learning about God, I reject that proposition based on a wealth of scriptural evidence, much of which we will explore in this opening chapter.

Of course, God does not have human emotions. He isn't subject to fickle feelings and whimsical moods, nor is He influenced unduly by the condition of the worlds He has created. You can be sure that He never experiences PMS (Prophetic Mood Swings)! God does not sit in heaven worrying over our earthly condition, wringing His hands with sweaty palms. I don't believe there is ever a conversation within the Godhead where something is said along the lines of, *"Oh My, what are We going to do?"*

Yet, in Scripture, we see that God "takes delight." He experiences gladness and joy. He is lavishly and lovingly generous. His protective instinct is often aroused, and He goes to battle on behalf of those in need. He comforts. He is sympathetic and relatable, tolerant and patient.

The Bible shows us how God expresses His emotions; Zephaniah even portrays Him as a singing God. Just look at the numerous words of emotion in these three different translations of Zephaniah 3:17, including the *New American Standard Bible*, which is the main version used in this book:

> *The LORD your God is in your midst, a victorious warrior. He will **exult** over you with **joy**, He will be **quiet** in His **love**, He will **rejoice** over you with **shouts of joy**.*

> *For the LORD your God is living among you. He is a mighty savior. He will take **delight** in you with **gladness**. With his **love**, he will **calm** all your fears. He will **rejoice** over you with **joyful songs**.*
>
> (NLT)

> *The LORD your God is with you, the Mighty Warrior who saves. He will take **great delight** in you; in his **love** he will no longer rebuke you, but will **rejoice** over you with **singing**.*   (NIV)

As human beings made in God's image, we have been created as emotional beings because that is the way He is. That is already a pretty clear acknowledgment that our Creator God is Himself an emotional Being. Due to our fallen state, we are also badly tainted with sin and rebellion and evil motives; yet, in our original design, we are modeled like our Creator. He expresses Himself in many ways, and He wants us to follow Him closely as we love and serve Him. He is not a distant, detached, aloof, and unfeeling God; indeed, He is passionate and compassionate.

THAT YOUR JOY MAY BE FULL

Look again at the Scripture quoted at the beginning of this chapter: *"These things I have spoken to you, that My joy may remain in you, and that your joy may be full"* (John 15:11 NKJV). This is Jesus, speaking to His disciples. Remember that He and the Father God are one; here, He is speaking as God, telling the disciples that His own joy is increasing as He is explaining the kingdom to them, and that He wants their joy to increase as well. He wants joy to be a shared emotion for all of His disciples, including present-day you and me.

See how He *longs* for us to share His joy:

*"Is Ephraim My dear son? Is he a delightful child? Indeed, as often as I have spoken against him, I certainly still remember him; therefore **My heart yearns** for him; I will surely have mercy on him,"*
declares the LORD.   (Jeremiah 31:20)

*How can I give you up, Ephraim? How can I hand you over, Israel? How can I make you like Admah? How can I set you like Zeboiim? **My heart churns** within Me; **My sympathy is stirred**.*
                                                       (Hosea 11:8 NKJV)

*So he got up and went to his father. But while he was still a long way off, his father saw him and was **filled with compassion** for him; he ran to his son, threw his arms around him and **kissed** him. The son said to him, "Father, I have sinned against heaven and against you. I am no longer worthy to be called your son." But the father said to his servants, "Quick! Bring the best robe and put it on him. Put a ring on his finger and sandals on his feet. Bring the fattened calf and kill it. Let's have a **feast and celebrate**."*   (Luke 15:20–23 NIV)

*For God so **loved** the world, that He gave His only begotten Son, that whoever believes in Him shall not perish, but have eternal life.*
                                                       (John 3:16)

To my way of thinking, none of these Scriptures portrays a cerebral, emotionless deity. No, together they give us a full-color picture of the

God who is moved by emotions such as yearning, love, and compassion to act. He loved the people He has created so much that He sent His only Son to save them from a well-deserved sentence of death. He loves each of us so much that He takes the initiative to save us even when we spurn Him repeatedly.

God's heart beats with such a profound depth of feelings that on a celestial EEG, it will never flatline. When we accept His outreaches and respond to His love, all of heaven throbs with joy and celebrates with Him. In fact, heaven knows how to throw a party!

GOD'S HEART BEATS WITH SUCH A PROFOUND DEPTH OF FEELINGS THAT ON A CELESTIAL EEG, IT WILL NEVER FLATLINE.

EMOTIONS IGNITED

Jonathan Edwards, colonial pastor, preacher, and theologian of the First Great Awakening (who from his portraits appears to represent stern formality and rigid fortitude), preached about what he called "holy affections," that is, sanctified emotions. He wrote, "True religion, in great part, consists in holy affections."[1] He considered the enjoyment of holy affections to be part of the abundant life of true believers. As Psalm 16:11 puts it, *"You will make known to me the path of life; in Your presence is fullness of joy; in Your right hand there are pleasures forever."*

Jack Hayford, respected elder statesman in the body of Christ, considers that in an environment in which God's Word is foundational and the person of Christ is the focus, His Holy Spirit brings clear thinking along with an emotional response. He says that the Spirit can be

1. Jonathan Edwards, *A Treatise Concerning Religious Affections* (1746), www.jonathan-edwards.org/religiousAffections.pdf, part I, page 6.

trusted to both "enlighten the intelligence and ignite the emotions."[2] Hayford explains that God is not asking anybody to abandon reason or to "succumb to some euphoric feeling."[3] Instead, He is asking us to surrender senseless fears about His control of both our intellects and our emotions.

An emotion, after all, happens to be a lively and vigorous activity of the mind, not a separate function outside the operation of the mind. Our emotions cannot be dissected from the other actions of our intellects. We are delighted or displeased with things all the time, and our emotions have an impact upon our bodies, our level of holiness, our relationships, our decisions. Whether we are being acknowledged for a job well done or reprimanded for a mistake, emotions can burst to the surface instantaneously—momentarily bypassing the more "logical thinking" part of us. How we handle those bursts are determining factors of our true emotional health.

In the context of our life in Christ, we can look to the Word of God to learn more about our emotions. For example, whenever we see the word *heart* in Scripture, we must be ready to consider our emotions within the context of the passage.

Over the years of ministering with people, I have realized that human hearts clearly can be hardened or softened toward the things of God. Jesus told the parable of the sower to alert us to the various conditions of the human heart:

> *Listen! A farmer went out to plant some seeds. As he scattered them across his field, some seeds fell on a footpath, and the birds came and ate them. Other seeds fell on shallow soil with underlying rock. The seeds sprouted quickly because the soil was shallow. But the plants soon wilted under the hot sun, and since they didn't have deep roots, they died. Other seeds fell among thorns that grew up and choked out the tender plants. Still other seeds fell on fertile soil, and they*

---

2. Jack Hayford, *A Passion for Fullness* (Waco, TX: Word Publishing, 1991), 31.
3. Ibid.

produced a crop that was thirty, sixty, and even a hundred times as
much as had been planted!   (Matthew 13:3–8 NLT)

What is the condition of your heart's "soil"? Is it rocky or thorny? Or is your heart like good, soft soil, ready to receive the Sower's seed? For years, I prayed, "Lord, send forth Your Word like a hammer to shatter the hard places in my heart." I believe this has been an important prayer that has helped me grow spiritually. It is good to have a sensitive heart and a soul that is responsive to the emotions of God as expressed through the powerful presence of His Holy Spirit. My prayer is based on the words of Jeremiah 23:29: "'Is not My word like fire?' declares the LORD, 'and like a hammer which shatters a rock?'"

Ultimately, all of God's actions and all of His emotions are rooted in one sweeping emotion—*love*. He expresses His love in so many personalized ways that we can spend our lifetimes trying to comprehend it. However, all of our efforts to grasp the length and breadth and height and depth of His love fall short, don't they? That is why we need to keep praying this prayer from Ephesians 3:

That Christ may dwell in [our] *hearts through faith; that* [we], *being*
rooted and grounded in love, may be able to comprehend with all the
saints what is the width and length and depth and height—to know
the love of Christ which passes knowledge; that [we] *may be filled*
with all the fullness of God.   (Ephesians 3:17–19 NKJV)

FEELING LOVED

Of course, it's one thing to be informed about God's love for us, but entirely another to fully believe it for yourself. Even if you can get (with His help) to the point that you really believe it, it goes to another dimension when you can *experience* feeling loved with sanctified emotions. I encourage you to seek this experience and to ask Him to heal and renew your emotions so that you can have more than a fleeting taste of His love.

I have no doubt you know firsthand that love is the most wonderful and complicated human emotion of all. Songs are sung, poems written, and sermons preached about it; lives are even lost because of it. So, we must always begin with a head knowledge of God's pure love. For this, clear teaching is all-important: *"You will know the truth, and the truth will set you free"* (John 8:32 NIV, NLT, TLB). Within the context of the body of Christ, every believer must probe the depths of the Word of God to learn more about His love.

Over time, we can gain a "heart revelation" concerning our head knowledge about God. This represents growth and maturity in our faith. The Word of God tells us we are loved, both individually and corporately, and we can "pray into" the Word, soaking ourselves in it by reading and rereading Scripture so that it becomes grafted into our hearts and minds.

As we ask for a spirit of wisdom and revelation to blow upon the written Word that has been stored up within us, the Father gives us tastes of love every day—almost every moment if we are open to His revelations. We experience for ourselves that He Himself is the Source of love and that He truly loves us better than any other, although He often uses other individuals to demonstrate His commitment to us.

ONE OF THE BEST FRUITS OF YOUR FAITH-FILLED MATURITY WILL BE YOUR RENEWED CAPACITY TO LOVE OTHERS.

Have you encountered, experienced, and absorbed the love of God for yourself? Have you seriously considered how much He rejoices over you—that He has passionate joy over knowing you have accepted His gift of salvation? Have you had an experiential revelation concerning your knowledge about His love? Do you know firsthand how fully accepted you are by the Beloved? If not, stop right now and ask the Holy Spirit to confirm to your heart what your head has come to believe. As He begins a new work in your mind and heart, you will be thrilled with all the blessings He has waiting for you to enjoy!

The fruit of the Holy Spirit, listed in the book of Galatians, is actually a list of emotions—the first of which is love—further evidence that God has emotions. One of the best fruits of your faith-filled maturity will be your renewed capacity to love others. You will find that you have grown in the fruit of the Spirit, which indicates you have grown in the emotional realm. *"The fruit of the Spirit is love, joy, peace, patience, kindness, goodness, faithfulness, gentleness, self-control"* (Galatians 5:22–23). You grow in wisdom when you live a fruitful lifestyle and know when and how to exercise the spirit of love.

My personal experience illustrates this growth and progression in emotional maturity. Although I grew up with a righteous inheritance from my mother's side, I experienced the negative impact of verbal abuse from my father's side. As a consequence, it was easier for me to relate to Jesus as my Lord and Savior and Friend than it was for me to relate to God, His Father, as my good Daddy. It took an encounter with the Holy Spirit to bring me into a renewed place of healing and security in the Father's love.

This personal "Father encounter" actually led to a dramatic reconciliation with my earthly father before he died, which further enhanced my relational ability to feel loved. My earthly father had barely tasted the love of God, having been woefully abused in his youth, yet he came into an experience of God's love much later in life before he went home to heaven.

When my father was in the hospital slipping away from kidney failure, he had a couple of startling dreams that majorly got his attention. He sent word through my mother asking for me to have a private time with him. He knew I might be able to help him understand these alarming dreams. But there was a problem: I was leaving for a prolonged trip to Cambodia and Thailand. So, my wife, Michal Ann, and I prayed that the Lord would sustain my dad. And God was faithful and did more than we expected.

By the time I returned from my extensive travels in Southeast Asia, my dad had rallied and been released from the hospital. As soon as I got home, I drove to my parents' house in rural Cowgill, Missouri. My mom stepped aside, allowing for a personal time between just my dad and me.

We both knew why I was there. My dad readily opened up his troubled soul and shared the dreams with me. I unpacked the dreams for him in such a manner that revealed the Lord's direct message for him—a message that required a response. The tangible presence of the Lord was undeniably with us. Afterward, this once very strong, private man became completely transparent with me, telling me stories of how he had been raised, abuse he had suffered, and things he had struggled with in life. This conversation was unlike any other I had previously had with this rather rough and tough man whom I'd grown up fearing.

But things changed that day. With all the courage he could muster, my dad said, "Son, how did you get so close to Jesus, anyway? Did you just press into God, or what?" I shared some of my personal story line, as well, and we really connected. He called me "Son." As far as I can remember, that was the very first time he had ever done so. I had never, ever, before felt celebrated as a son; I had felt merely tolerated.

We talked and prayed together, and for the first time, I addressed him as "Father." Tears flowed down his cheeks as we held hands and blessed each other. For both of us, the love of our Father God became real as never before. Both of us had felt like orphans, even though we were not; but that day, we came to know, deep down, the truth that we hold a special place in God's heart and a special place in each other's hearts.

After that, I became a better father myself. People who did not know what had occurred came up to me and said things like, "It feels like you are a father now. You're not just a teacher or an instructor, but also a spiritual father to others." That was so good to hear. Personal growth is a process—an *upward* process. My heart and emotive feeler realm were now more complete. I now "felt loved," not just tolerated.

Many people grow up with some type of love deficiency stemming from verbal abuse, physical abuse, neglect, divorce, death, or another cause. Some turn inward, and their emotional capacity is limited. Others turn outward to false sources of love. All struggle. Feeling more and more secure in Father God's love is a lifelong process. Similarly, a happy couple stares lovingly into each other's eyes as they stand before God, friends, and family on their wedding day, but maintaining and refreshing that love requires a lifelong commitment.

As we keep recognizing, accepting, and growing in God's love, may we say, with Mike Bickle (whom I've heard preach about this passionate love of God from Song of Solomon more than anybody I know), "I'm His *favorite*." Far from being arrogant, such a confidence stems from a deep, experiential knowledge of the unlimited, passionate love of the God who is big enough to treat every individual as His personal favorite. Oh, by the way, I now believe that I am God's favorite, also, and so are you! Our Father God has a special place at His table waiting just for you.

EXPERIENCING THE ECSTASY OF HIS PRESENCE

In the fourth verse of Psalm 27, David states that there is only *"one thing"* that he desires: *"One thing I have desired of the LORD, that will I seek: that I may dwell in the house of the LORD all the days of my life, to behold the beauty of the LORD, and to inquire in His temple"* (NKJV). Above wealth and health and fame, David simply wants to be—24/7—in the presence of the Lord.

Do you echo David's desire to continually be in your Father's presence? We who know the truth about God's omnipresence (see, for example, Matthew 28:20) want to respond to James's instruction in the first part of James 4:8: *"Draw near to God and He will draw near to you"* (NKJV). We believe that the very atmosphere, the air we breathe, is different in His presence. We expect our hearts to leap with joy—excited to be enveloped within His embrace. As the psalmist says:

> How lovely is your dwelling place, Lord Almighty! My soul yearns, even faints, for the courts of the Lord; my heart and my flesh cry out for the living God. Even the sparrow has found a home, and the swallow a nest for herself, where she may have her young—a place near your altar, Lord Almighty, my King and my God. Blessed are those who dwell in your house; they are ever praising you.
> (Psalm 84:1–4 NIV)

The words of that psalm are inscribed on the headstone of my dear late wife because they summarize the goal of her life; and as long as I live, I want that to be the goal of my life too. Michal Ann exhibited a Psalm 84 lifestyle, and everyone who knew her saw that she walked her talk. So, now, I recommend this passage as a good prayer for you to pray for yourself as well.

THERE WAS ONLY ONE MOSES AND ONE DAVID; BUT EVEN IN OUR ORDINARY, EVERYDAY LIVES, WE CAN FOLLOW THEIR EXAMPLE IN OUR PASSIONATE PURSUIT OF GOD.

When we express our desire for God's presence, He responds lovingly. Like the father of the prodigal son, our heavenly Father is already running toward us before we can see Him. As we turn toward Him in worship, especially when we worship Him in the company of others in the body of Christ, He personally comes to each of us. God basks in our worship and praise, as we know He is worthy of all glory. He welcomes our personal and our corporate thanksgiving and adoration.

Moses knew how crucial it is to experience the presence of God, without whom he never could have hoped to accomplish anything:

> *"Now therefore, I pray You, if I have found favor in Your sight, let me know Your ways that I may know You, so that I may find favor in Your sight. Consider too, that this nation is Your people." And He said, "My presence shall go with you, and I will give you rest." Then he said to Him, "If Your presence does not go with us, do not lead us up from here. For how then can it be known that I have found favor in Your sight, I and Your people? Is it not by Your going with us, so that we, I and Your people, may be distinguished from all the other people who are upon the face of the earth?" The* LORD *said to Moses, "I will also do this thing of which you have spoken; for you have found favor in My sight and I have known you by name." Then Moses said, "I pray You, show me Your glory!" And He said, "I Myself will make all My goodness pass before you, and will proclaim the name of the* LORD *before you."* (Exodus 33:13–19)

The glory of God was made manifest to Moses, as Moses had desired. And so it can be with us, regardless of the magnitude of the call before us. There was only one Moses and one David; but even in our ordinary, everyday lives, we can follow their example in our passionate pursuit of God. Yes, you, too, can experience the ecstasy of His presence.

A HEART THAT BURNS

Do you feel celebrated by God, special to Him? Or do you think and feel that He merely tolerates you? When you pray, do you enjoy your time with the Lord, or does your time with Him seem like an endurance contest? Do you struggle with a sense of rejection and dejection—or do you know moments of elation? Your emotions indicate what your whole being needs and wants: a never-ending embrace from your Father in heaven.

Remember the sequence of wholeness in God: First, you gain knowledge about His love from reading His Word, the Bible. Next, you move into a revelation of His love, which enables you to experience the passionate emotions God expresses toward you—emotions that restore you. Then, at last, you can express your genuine love toward Him. And because you are so secure in His love, you are now capable of loving the people around you.

Are you like one of the disciples on the road to Emmaus? When they encountered the risen Lord Jesus, they didn't recognize Him. However, their hearts knew who this Traveler was. Their hearts burned within them: *"Were not our hearts burning within us while He was speaking to us on the road, while He was explaining the Scriptures to us?"* (Luke 24:32).

With Jesus walking alongside you and His Holy Spirit within you, I pray that your heart will burn with bright flames of love. With a burning heart, proceed along your life's journey immersed in His very Word of life and carrying His presence wherever He may lead you.

PRAYER OF A PASSIONATE HEART

Father, in Jesus's great name, I am so thankful that, through the work of His cross, I can come into a living and vibrant relationship with You, my loving heavenly Father. What a delight and privilege it is to participate in daily communication with the God of the universe, and how amazing it is to feel Your love! What a revelation it is to know that You are the God who shares Your exhilarating emotions with me as one of Jesus's followers. All praise to You, the living, loving Lord! Amen.

2

Your Natural and Spiritual Senses

"For everyone who partakes only of milk is not accustomed to the word of righteousness, for he is an infant.
But solid food is for the mature, who because of practice have their senses trained to discern good and evil."
—Hebrews 5:13–14

Of course, you know that infants drink milk, and that as they mature, they move on to solid food. They progress from baby food to peanut butter sandwiches to steaks and (hopefully) broccoli. Still, almost everybody likes to wash down their cookies with a glass of milk. In the same way, we learn to chew on the solid food of the kingdom of God, but we wash it down with the basic truths of the gospel.

From time to time, we need to review those truths, don't we? Then we can get more out of the richer food that sustains our growth toward maturity. And as the above passage from Hebrews explains, chewing (pondering) on that solid food on a daily basis is what trains our senses to discern the difference between good and evil: "*...the mature, who* **because of practice** *have their senses trained to discern good and evil.*" We must *practice* the gospel truth in all of its implications. We must ingest the food of the gospel and move forward in the strength that it provides. Practicing is the key.

By way of example, I think of my daughter-in-law, Pearl, who is an accomplished violinist and pianist. When she performs a piece of music, she has the whole score memorized and plays it flawlessly. But, prior to the performance, she practices. She started playing the piano when she was about six years old, and she has been practicing daily ever since. She has dedicated herself to her training. A good part of her flawless performance is due to practice, practice, practice.

At this point, you might expect me to say, "Practice makes perfect." But that is not really our goal with spiritual discernment and maturity, is it? (Besides, our Christian life is not a performance.) Where our spiritual lives are concerned, absolute perfection is too high of a goal; it will constantly elude us. Always remember, advancing is our goal, going from glory to glory. (See 2 Corinthians 3:18.)

But our *purpose* is not elusive. To become spiritually mature, we must continually grow, year after year, into the purposes God has for our lives. And the only way to keep growing, to keep increasing in maturity, is to keep chewing on, swallowing, and digesting God's Word, moving in its supernatural strength to obey His divine commands.

TRAINING OUR SENSES

According to the passage from Hebrews 5, our *senses*—both our natural senses and our spiritual senses—are being developed when we practice: "*...who because of practice have their senses trained to discern good and evil.*"

What is meant by our "senses," from both a natural point of view and a spiritual one?

First off, we have five natural senses: (1) sight, (2) hearing, (3) touch, (4) taste, and (5) smell. I think it is helpful to add a sixth sense, "knowing," because our mind is trained to interpret all of the information that comes to it via our other five senses. Sight involves the eyes, of course; hearing, the ears; touch, the external "feelers" of our body; taste, the tongue; smell, the nose; and knowing, the mind. (For more teaching on this subject, see my book *The Discerner*.[4])

These physical senses correspond to spiritual senses as follows:

1. Eyes (seeing): visions and dreams

2. Ears (hearing): voices and sounds

3. Heart (feeling): emotions and feelings

4. Tongue (tasting): good and evil

5. Nose (smelling): good and bad

6. Mind (knowing): divine thoughts and impressions

Years ago, I learned from John Wimber, the late leader of the worldwide Association of Vineyard Churches, that we are to "give expression to the impression." We are meant to learn how to interpret the messages (the impressions) that come to our minds and hearts via both our natural and our spiritual senses. We can mature into knowing what even the slightest impressions indicate and also into knowing what to do with them. After all, messages from God do not always come like lightning bolts. In fact, they rarely do.

Most of the time, we receive only slight impressions. As we learn to surrender our senses—all of them, natural and spiritual alike—to the direction of the Holy Spirit, we can give a comprehensible expression to them. It will always be a process of *learning from doing*. Our "practicing" is more like experimentation.

This works differently for every person. In my experience, I receive a lot of input through my spiritual eyes and ears, and my feelings. My ability to perceive has improved over the years. When I first became a

4. *The Discerner: Hearing, Confirming, and Acting on Prophetic Revelation* (New Kensington, PA: Whitaker House, 2017).

Christian, I used to see and hear things as if they were coming to me on an old black-and-white TV. I was limited as to what I could receive within my little conservative box. I was quite sensitive, but I was not yet empowered spiritually—and I wasn't giving my senses practice in discernment.

Then, when I was about twenty years old, I was baptized in the Holy Spirit, and I began to overflow with His presence and gifts. First, I began to move in the gift of prophecy. After this, I began to pray, speak, and worship in the gift of tongues. It was as if my life went from that little old black-and-white TV to a large-screen, full-color TV overnight. I went from being a sensitive young man—often oversensitive to negative things—to being quick to sense God's thoughts and feelings through the senses and impressions He was sending me. Everything became alive and vibrant.

What made such a difference? I should rephrase: *Who* made such a difference? The Holy Spirit. At last, it seemed that I was moving from milk to solid food, setting myself on a course of study and practice. This was my life purpose, and God continued to guide me along the way: *"For we are His workmanship, created in Christ Jesus for good works, which God prepared beforehand that we should walk in them"* (Ephesians 2:10 NKJV).

You and I have been made in the image and likeness of the triune God: Father, Son, and Holy Spirit. We are triune beings: spirit, soul, and body. We mirror our Creator more fully than any other part of His creation. With surrender, practice, and training, we can fulfill His purposes for our lives, illuminating the darkness by reflecting His light wherever we go.

Our goal is to become supernaturally natural. We want to be as effective as possible in our service and in ministry to and for the Lord Jesus Christ. We want to be obedient to His wishes. The single best way to maximize our effectiveness is to learn how to use all of our senses. That means using both our physical and spiritual eyes, our physical and spiritual ears, and so on. Having started out in life learning how to use our physical senses, we adopt a new spiritual way of operating, with the ever-present help of the Holy Spirit.

Scripture actually lays out the fact that our spiritual senses come along after we have practiced using our physical senses for a time. The apostle Paul wrote to the Corinthian believers, *"The spiritual did not come first, but the natural, and after that the spiritual"* (1 Corinthians 15:46 NIV). Over time, we can become naturally supernatural and supernaturally natural. We can encounter something with our natural senses and then tune in to God, who interprets it for us and clues us in to the spiritual interpretation.

> *THE SINGLE BEST WAY TO MAXIMIZE OUR EFFECTIVENESS IS TO LEARN HOW TO USE ALL OF OUR SENSES. THAT MEANS USING BOTH OUR PHYSICAL AND SPIRITUAL EYES, OUR PHYSICAL AND SPIRITUAL EARS, AND SO ON.*

SURRENDERING YOUR SENSES

It only makes "sense" to recognize that the only way to be naturally supernatural is to surrender our natural *senses* to the Lord. We must dedicate our whole selves—body, mind, and spirit—to His service and for His use and His glory. This process is called *consecration*, which means setting something apart for a particular purpose, or to God. When we consecrate our whole selves to God, we must permit Him to be completely in charge. Otherwise, He isn't free to minister through us. Full consecration on our part is what it takes for Him to become the *Lord* of our lives, not only our Savior—as important as that role also is.

Our default setting is to continue running our own lives, which, sadly, never leads us into a righteous, joyous, Spirit-filled life. In his Roman epistle, Paul urges believers away from continuing to live in the impurity of their fallen humanity and on toward full consecration to God:

> *Do not offer any part of yourself to sin as an instrument of wick-edness, but rather offer yourselves to God as those who have been brought from death to life; and offer every part of yourself to him as an instrument of righteousness.... I am using an example from everyday life because of your human limitations. Just as you used to offer yourselves as slaves to impurity and to ever-increasing wicked-ness, so now offer yourselves as slaves to righteousness leading to holi-ness.... Therefore, I urge you, brothers and sisters, in view of God's mercy, to offer your bodies as a living sacrifice, holy and pleasing to God—this is your true and proper worship. Do not conform to the pattern of this world, but be transformed by the renewing of your mind. Then you will be able to test and approve what God's will is—his good, pleasing and perfect will.*
> (Romans 6:13, 19; 12:1–2 NIV)

The transforming renewal of the Spirit happens in your mind, which is the seat of your obedience to God's will. As you move forward as a "slave to righteousness leading to holiness," sanctification occurs. Your will becomes sanctified and gets set apart as holy unto God. It is a one-to-one transaction that never happens automatically. Responding to the Holy Spirit's invitation, you have to personally present your spirit, soul, and body to God so that His power can purify and hallow you, thus bridging the gap between the natural and the supernatural.

When you consecrate your whole self to God, of necessity that includes your natural senses—your sight, hearing, touch or feeling, taste, smell, and your sense of knowing. It is only through the shed blood of our Lord Jesus Christ that you and I are able to do this. I mention this in case you think that an in-depth consecration of your innermost being is something you can achieve by virtue of your own human strength. We need God for everything, and in everything He gets all the glory.

Consecration is far more than a onetime transaction—it comes with step-by-step upgrades. In biblical language, each believer goes "*from glory to glory."* We don't have to stay at the same level. In the past, we may have been stuck, but now we can grow into the present and future. *"We all, with unveiled face, beholding as in a mirror the glory of the Lord, are being transformed into the same image from glory to glory, just as from the Lord, the Spirit"* (2 Corinthians 3:18).

GROWING AND MATURING

Every time you reaffirm the consecration of your temple—your entire body, mind, and spirit—it is an act of worship to God. He takes your offering and transforms it. What does that actually look like?

Let's say you present your eyes to Him. By doing so, you are purposefully choosing to not look at anything impure, such as pornography. You are bending your will to the will of the Lord, the Righteous One. You want your inner eyes to behold the things of His kingdom, so you intentionally keep looking in His direction. Over time, as you seek Him, He will give you visions. His Spirit will help you understand what you are seeing, and you will learn a new way of using your supernaturally natural eyes.

The cleansing and empowering are God's part, after you have done your part by presenting your eyesight to Him. He enables you to cooperate with Him because He is faithful. You know that He always completes the work He has started. (See, for example, Philippians 1:6.)

By the way, don't give up just because you sometimes fail to cooperate with Him. Everybody falls and fails. But be reassured that, if and when you fall, you *can* get back up. The righteous men and women of God are resilient; they may fall seven times, but they always get back up again. (See Proverbs 24:16.) We are the comeback kids, thanks to our saving Lord. Just return to Him, humbled and repentant, and ask Him to help you get up again. He will help you. He will empower you once again with His Holy Spirit. He will wash you off. He will lead you back to the Word of God and to the blood of Jesus. He will buoy you up, reminding you that no one is perfect—but that we all can be perfected. (See, for example, 1 Peter 5:10.)

After all, each one of us is a child, even after we have become more "mature." Most children crawl before they can walk, and they walk before they can run. Nobody can start off running straight out of the womb. It takes practice, along with a lot of falling, crying, and getting back up.

For example, where your eyes are concerned, you may say to God:

Lord, I present my eyes to You as Your servants. I confess that, in the past, I have surrendered them to unrighteousness, but now I renounce my sin and ask for Your forgiveness. I ask for Your supernatural grace. You are faithful and just to forgive me of my sins and to cleanse me from all unrighteousness. Now, please cleanse my eye gate, which I have sullied by my actions. Cleanse me in the seat of my emotions from the natural effects of what I have done. I surrender my eyes to You once again, and I ask You to help me shut them to sin and open them to the things of God. Amen.

We need to keep close to God so that we can mature. His Spirit does not need to mature in us; we need to mature in Him. You may have heard it said that there is no such thing as a "baby Holy Spirit" or a "junior Holy Spirit" for the young in Christ, the immature ones. Any hindrances to your faith and spiritual maturity that you may encounter are not due to a lack on the part of the Holy Spirit but rather due to a lack in your consecration and dedication to Him in His unlimited strength. Unlike spiritual gifting, Christlike character—the fruit of the Spirit—never comes fully developed.

God wants you to mature in your ability to discern both good and evil. By that, I mean discerning good *from* evil, not so much good *versus* evil. This is a somewhat subtle distinction. We need to see, smell, feel, and know whether what we are encountering is good or evil, and, subsequently, to know what to do with our discernment—how to respond.

The bottom line: God desires to manifest Himself through us, and He does so to whatever degree we allow Him to take the reins of our lives. The Godhead expresses Himself in such a variety of ways that human beings cannot catalog them all. He manifests Himself through the individuals He has created for His glory; no one is left out.

How exciting to know that, from time to time, there are defining moments that change everything. Such strategic moments often point us toward God's big direction for our life's journey. Defining moments are different for each believer, and some believers will experience multiple such moments during their lifetimes. Some of these defining moments may occur early in life or later, some in times of crisis and others in times of tranquility. Invite Him to demonstrate His glory through you, and then just see what He will do!

> **THE GODHEAD EXPRESSES HIMSELF IN SUCH A VARIETY OF WAYS THAT HUMAN BEINGS CANNOT CATALOG THEM ALL. HE MANIFESTS HIMSELF THROUGH THE INDIVIDUALS HE HAS CREATED FOR HIS GLORY; NO ONE IS LEFT OUT.**

A PERSONAL DEFINING MOMENT

In the 1980s, I began a personal fast as I sought the Lord for greater intimacy with Christ. I was in full-time pastoral ministry at Harvest Fellowship in Warrensburg, Missouri, and Michal Ann and I had a small house in a rural subdivision. During this fast, the Holy Spirit whispered to me that He had some surprises He wanted to show me. For five consecutive nights, the Spirit awakened me at two in the morning. I responded by going out into our little living room and simply sitting on our couch to watch and wait.

Each night, it seemed, a different sense was being highlighted by the Holy Spirit. The first night, He drew near to me by speaking to me, opening up my hearing. Another time, I felt a heat or flame sitting on my chest, granting me a heart on fire. But what I remember the most was what transpired on the fifth consecutive night of waiting and watching with the Lord. It truly was a surprise package!

That night, I was wide awake once again at two in the morning, waiting with eager anticipation, when things changed. The atmosphere in the living room shifted. I could feel the Holy Spirit's manifest presence drawing near. I sensed angelic activity. Then everything went still. Silence, golden silence. Heaven seemed to invade my space.

In an open vision, a gift package floated down from heaven above and landed right in my lap. The gift was wrapped in gold foil paper complete with red ribbon tied in a magnificent bow. I knew this was a personal gift from the Holy Spirit and that I was to open God's precious present with care. I proceeded to untie the ribbon and then prayerfully lifted the lid from the box.

I thought, "What am I supposed to do next?" I had never done something like this before. I had never read a manual on "How to Open a Present from God." So, I leaned into the voice of my heart and went with the flow.

I slowly reached down inside the box and touched two round objects that felt unusual. I grasped these two objects, one in each hand, and carefully brought them up out of the box. What do you think I was given on that fifth night? To my shock and surprise, I felt, held, and saw two "eyes." They were the eyes of a seer. By faith, I received those eyes as a gift and a calling from the Father above.

With consecration, I brought both of my hands up to my face and placed the eyes of the seer into my body that night. Yes, I was already moving in a visionary capacity to some degree at this point in time. But from that night onward, I experienced an increase in my level of sensitivity, my clarity, and my confidence in seeing, feeling, and knowing. This was a defining moment for my life and ministry. And it came in the midst of a time of personal consecration.

EMPOWERING YOUR SENSES

Any Spirit-filled follower of Christ Jesus can learn to walk in spiritual gifts and Spirit-empowered senses. God does not use only an elite group of "special forces" to do His work. First Corinthians 12:4–7 makes this clear:

Now there are varieties of gifts, but the same Spirit. And there are varieties of ministries, and the same Lord. There are varieties of effects, but the same God who works all things in all persons. But to each one is given the manifestation of the Spirit for the common good.

Paul writes that God works *all* things in *all* persons, and to *each one* has been given the manifestation of the Spirit for the common good. That includes you, regardless of your starting place or your current level of spiritual maturity. We all need to grasp the fact that we have been called to greater things, and we all need to pursue the spiritual gifts—which very often will incorporate our Spirit-infused, naturally supernatural senses.

The spiritual gifts that God has given His people make us interdependent. We need each other in the body of Christ, and we need to keep flowing with the same Spirit. In the next few verses of 1 Corinthians 12, Paul continues his explanation of how this works:

For to one is given the word of wisdom through the Spirit, to another the word of knowledge through the same Spirit, to another faith by the same Spirit, to another gifts of healings by the same Spirit, to another the working of miracles, to another prophecy, to another discerning of spirits, to another different kinds of tongues, to another the interpretation of tongues. But one and the same Spirit works all these things, distributing to each one individually as He wills.

(1 Corinthians 12:8–11 NKJV)

The gift of discerning of spirits (see verse 10) is especially valuable. This gift is the supernatural ability to distinguish or perceive what spirit is behind a particular manifestation or activity. It helps us to differentiate between the activity and inspiration of the Holy Spirit, angels, demons, and the human spirit—the hidden motivations of a person's heart or spirit, including our own. We know that the gift refers to this ability to distinguish the root sources of thoughts and decisions because the term *"spirits"* is plural.

Even the definition of *discern* indicates a deciding, a distinguishing between things, a passing of sentence upon a situation. When the gift of discerning of spirits is activated, we consider with healthy skepticism something dubious that has been presented to us, having sensed question marks (the helpful kind) in our spirits. Something inside us says, "Wait a moment. Something's not right here. What is it, and where does it come from?"

> **WITH CONSECRATED GIFTS AND SENSES, WE CAN REACH OUT TO THE BODY OF CHRIST AND TO THE WORLD AT LARGE IN BOTH SPIRITUAL AND PRACTICAL WAYS.**

The discerning of spirits is a large part of what this book is about.[5] It is to your benefit to learn how to lean in toward the Holy Spirit and how to listen to the subtle senses that may not even capture your attention if you don't happen to recognize them as helpful. I want to help you fine-tune your "feeler" and your "knower" so that you will not have to keep groping around in the dark or being buffeted by the invisible influences surrounding you. You can test the spiritual atmosphere to see whether it comes from God and then take hold of your discernments, applying each for divine wisdom so you can decide what to do with them.

---

5. While *The Feeler* stands alone, I wrote it to complement my earlier book *The Discerner*. See the previous footnote for publication details.

With consecrated gifts and senses, we can reach out to the body of Christ and to the world at large in both spiritual and practical ways. We will be naturally supernatural. And supernaturally natural. We will be practically spiritual. And spiritually practical. Now that's the idea!

In spite of what some streams of the church declare—that the spiritual gifts ceased with the closing of the canon of Scripture and the death of the original apostles—the Holy Spirit, who is the same yesterday, today, and forever (see Hebrews 13:8), is still actively promulgating His gifts and graces. I believe in that truth so passionately that I have staked my entire ministry on it.

OUT OF THE HEART

Scripture says, *"Above all else, guard your heart, for everything you do flows from it"* (Proverbs 4:23 NIV). Therefore, those of us who want to have pure hearts that belong wholly to God must first recognize how sin hardens our hearts (see Hebrews 3:13) and then ask God to use His Word like a hammer on our hearts (see Jeremiah 23:29). Think about it: God is the only One who can enable us to obey His commandment to *"love not the world"* (1 John 2:15 KJV). Only by His grace can we be cleansed from all unrighteousness. (See 2 Corinthians 7:1; 1 John 1:9.) So, we fix our hope on God alone:

> *Beloved, now we are children of God; and it has not yet been revealed what we shall be, but we know that when He is revealed, we shall be like Him, for we shall see Him as He is. And everyone who has this hope in Him purifies himself, just as He is pure.*
>
> (1 John 3:2–3 NKJV)

Let's personalize this promise. God will cleanse your heart so that you can continue to walk in newness of life in the power of the Holy Spirit, and He will guide you into His truth. God loves you and has called you to serve Him obediently and with great joy. Offer your senses to Him as often as you need to. Practice using the spiritual gifts He has given you, and let Him teach you how to expand into the new realm of using your natural senses for supernatural purposes. You will no longer be a slave to sin but rather a captive of the Holy Spirit.

You may decide to pray over the condition of your heart on an annual basis, as I do. This is one of my habits, especially at the first of each Hebrew year,[6] and at other times interspersed throughout the year. Check for "heart problems" such as self-rejection or unforgiveness or fear of authority or fear of others' opinions of you. Ask the Holy Spirit to thaw the frozen places in your heart. Read the Word and apply it to your own life. It really works: *"You **will** know the truth, and the truth **will** set you free"* (John 8:32 NIV, NLT, TLB).

Ask yourself, "Have I been responding with the appropriate level of spiritual sensitivity, or have I been over- or underreacting out of my soul?" Let God into your heart. Give Him free rein. He is not only your loving Redeemer and Savior but also your caring, powerful Lord and Shepherd.

PRAYER OF A PASSIONATE HEART

Father, I surrender my natural senses to You. I desire to glorify You in all things. Therefore, I present and consecrate the members of my body for Your purposes and use. I give You my heart so that life will flow into it and out of it. I ask You to send the power of Your Spirit upon me. As You descend upon me, grace my sense of touch, my feelings, and my emotions with Your presence and power and gifting. At the end of the day, I want to give all glory to You. In Jesus's magnificent name, amen!

---

6. Rosh Hashanah, which is usually celebrated in September or October.

3

Jesus and the Heart of Compassion

"Jesus, moved with compassion, stretched out His hand and touched [a leprous man], and said to him, 'I am willing; be cleansed.'"
—Mark 1:41 (NKJV)

If you are going to walk in the redemptive nature of God in the Feeler realm, then it is imperative that you be rooted and motivated by authentic compassion. I am not talking about having just a gushy sense of urgency that pushes you into having to fix people and situations. I am talking about the necessity of knowing how to discern the true heart of Jesus, which compels us by the love of God to take action. The credit goes to Him—not us. If it points to us, it's just fake and manufactured.

The above verse from the first chapter of Mark does not give us a picture of Jesus looking down in scorn at the leprous man who had begged Him for healing. Jesus did not wave His hand dismissively and say, "Of course. I am God Almighty. Be healed!" His absolute power and capa-bility were not the reason He was willing to heal the leper; rather, the reason was His kindhearted sympathy. The God-Man Jesus was moved with heartfelt *compassion* to reach out and say, "*I am willing; be cleansed.*" Just seeing the man's condition and hearing his plea for help made Jesus quick to release him from his disfiguring disease.

Compassion counts for so much. It builds the bridge to carry the cargo. Look for it when you're not certain how to pray or what to say. If you can feel the compassion of Jesus rising up in your spirit, you can depend on the efficacy of your prayers because compassion-based prayers always find a swift answer.

COMPASSION IN THE BIBLE

Compassion is the sympathetic consciousness of the distress of others, along with a desire to mitigate or alleviate that distress. It's not quite the same as *empathy*, which is the ability to feel another person's pain, without the added desire to reach out in some way to make that pain better. Compassion leads to action. That's how it works with God, and that's how it ought to work with us.

If you were to do a biblical study on the theme of compassion, you would find that compassion is one of the defining characteristics of our loving God. In addition to other passages we will look at throughout this chapter, here are several examples:

> *The* Lord *is good to all; he has compassion on all he has made.*
> (Psalm 145:9 niv)

> *Seeing the people, [Jesus] felt compassion for them, because they were distressed and dispirited like sheep without a shepherd. Then He said to His disciples, "The harvest is plentiful, but the workers are few. Therefore beseech the Lord of the harvest to send out work-ers into His harvest."* (Matthew 9:36–38)

> *Now it happened, the day after, that [Jesus] went into a city called Nain; and many of His disciples went with Him, and a large crowd.*

And when He came near the gate of the city, behold, a dead man was being carried out, the only son of his mother; and she was a widow. And a large crowd from the city was with her. When the Lord saw her, He had compassion on her and said to her, "Do not weep." Then He came and touched the open coffin, and those who carried him stood still. And He said, "Young man, I say to you, arise." So he who was dead sat up and began to speak. And He presented him to his mother. (Luke 7:11–15 NKJV)

What moves God's heart with compassion? Simply the helpless, distressed state of someone (or some*thing*, we learn from Psalm 145). Instead of standing in judgment when He sees that one of His precious sheep is bewildered, harassed, or in trouble, God is filled with tender mercy that stirs Him to extend a helping hand.

The New Testament uses a large number of synonyms for *compassion* that are drawn from several key Greek words.[7] The verb *splanchnizomai* is often used to describe Jesus's compassionate reaction to suffering. It refers to being "moved as to one's inwards," or *splanchna*, "with compassion," or "to yearn with compassion." This is the word that is used in Mark 1:41 at the beginning of this chapter, and also in Matthew 9:36; 14:14; 15:32; 18:27; 20:34; Mark 6:34; 8:2; and Luke 7:13; 10:33; 15:20.

WHAT MOVES GOD'S HEART WITH COMPASSION? SIMPLY THE HELPLESS, DISTRESSED STATE OF SOMEONE OR SOMETHING.

Additionally, we find the verb *oikteiro* (a feeling of pity or distress because of the ills of others), which is used to describe God's compassion

7. Transliterations and definitions of Greek words in this section are taken from W. E. Vine, *Vine's Expository Dictionary of New Testament Words*, 1940, entry for "Compassion, Compassionate," https://www.studylight.org/dictionaries/ved/c/compassion-compassionate.html. Public domain.

in Romans 9:15 (where Paul is quoting Exodus 33:19): "[God] *says to Moses, 'I will have mercy on whomever I will have mercy, and I will have compassion on whomever I will have compassion'*" (NKJV).

In several places, the word *sumpatheo*, from which we derive the word *sympathy*, appears. It means "to suffer with another," "to be affected similarly," and "to have 'compassion' upon." It is found in Hebrews 4:15, which reads, *"For we do not have a high priest who cannot sympathize with our weaknesses, but One who has been tempted in all things as we are, yet without sin."* (See also Hebrews 10:34 regarding having sympathy for those in prison as if suffering with them.) The adjective form of the word, *sumpathes*, is translated *"compassionate"* in this verse: *"Finally, all of you, be like-minded, be sympathetic, love one another, be compassionate and humble"* (1 Peter 3:8 NIV).

The word *eleeo* is rendered "have compassion" in some translations of Matthew 18:33, in Mark 5:19, and in Jude 1:22. *Eleeo* carries the sense of having mercy or showing kindness by beneficence or assistance. Among the remaining "compassion" words in the New Testament, we have a couple of nouns: *oiktirmos* and *splanchnon*. Like its verb counterpart, the noun *oiktirmos* indicates a visceral response to perceived pain, that is, from the heart, the seat of emotion. We see it in Philippians 2:1, Colossians 3:12, and (translated as *"mercies"* or *"mercy"*) Romans 12:1, 2 Corinthians 1:3, and Hebrews 10:28. Paul advises all disciples, *"Therefore, as God's chosen people, holy and dearly loved, clothe yourselves with compassion"* (Colossians 3:12 NIV) or, as the *New American Standard Bible* translates it, *"...put on a heart of compassion."*

JESUS'S HEART OF COMPASSION

Jesus shows us the Father's heart of compassion by His words and actions. In our book *A Call to Compassion*, my late wife, Michal Ann, wrote the following:

If you have compassion, you will be moved to take action, as Jesus always did and still does. God wants you to know His compassion, receive His compassion, live His compassion, and share His compassion with others.… He is your loving heavenly Father, and He wants you to share in His compassion.[8]

Author and teacher Ken Blue wrote about Jesus's compassion in his book *Authority to Heal* because, so often, when Scripture describes one of Jesus's healing miracles, the story includes the fact that Jesus's heart was moved by compassion to heal: "The kind of compassion Jesus was said to have for people was not merely an expression of His will but rather an eruption from deep within His being. Out of this compassion of Jesus sprang His mighty works of rescue, healing, and deliverance."[9]

That's an amazing statement: compassion was "an eruption from deep within His being." To describe it as an "eruption" matches the powerful results of His ministry. Now, when you or I find ourselves confronted with a situation of need, and we experience even a scant tremor of compassion, let's be sure to notice it and act on it, as the Holy Spirit leads. Jesus's strong compassion is still flowing today—through people like us who will share His love with others. Let's look on every act of compassion as an opportunity to help others in His name, and to expand our capacity to love.

If you are a born-again, Spirit-filled believer, Jesus is alive and well in you. He dwells in your heart and wants you to receive His compassion for yourself—and to share it with others for their benefit. For those of us who consider ourselves "Feelers," cultivating the lifestyle of Jesus is our goal. We want to feel what He feels. We want to be moved by what moves God. Religious judgmentalism never works. We must allow the Holy Spirit to import the mercy and love of God within us so that we have something authentic to export.

GOD'S COMPASSION TOWARD US

You can't share Jesus's compassion unless you first experience it in your own life. Again, Jesus wants you to receive His compassion for

---

8. James Goll and Michal Ann Goll, *A Call to Compassion: Taking God's Unfailing Love to Your World* (Racine, WI: BroadStreet Publishing Group, 2016), 32.
9. Ken Blue, *Authority to Heal* (Downers Grove, IL: InterVarsity Press, 1987), 76–77.

yourself. What does that look like? How can you best open your heart to receive His compassion?

You can start by reviewing what you know about His nature and then asking yourself, "Who is God to me?" If you believe that it is in God's nature to care for His children and to heal them, then you will be closer to receiving His nurture and healing for yourself, so that you can then pass them on to others. If you believe that God hears prayers and answers them, you will be closer to knowing the reality of that interchange in your own life. If you believe that God acts on the basis of His compassionate, merciful nature, you will be more likely to not only receive His mercies and lovingkindness, but also turn your heart toward others and release the same.

Does God really care—for *you*? Can you trust Him? How has He demonstrated His care for you? How will He care for you today? You will receive based on what you believe.

You can read the Scriptures with compassion in mind. As we've noted, from beginning to end, the Word is filled with the revelation of God's compassionate nature. Even as He is a firm Judge, He is also, as the psalmist writes, filled with compassion:

> But He, being **full of compassion**, forgave their iniquity, and did not destroy them. Yes, many a time He turned His anger away, and did not stir up all His wrath; for He remembered that they were but flesh, a breath that passes away and does not come again.
>
> (Psalm 78:38–39 NKJV)

READ THE SCRIPTURES WITH COMPASSION IN MIND. FROM BEGINNING TO END, THE WORD IS FILLED WITH THE REVELATION OF GOD'S COMPASSIONATE NATURE.

God turns away His anger—actually quite justifiable anger—and gives us second and third chances. It is His nature: *"But thou, O Lord, art a God full of compassion, and gracious, long suffering, and plenteous in mercy and truth"* (Psalm 86:15 KJV). Make the effort to confess, out loud, what you believe, saying, "Lord, You are a God of compassion. You are gracious toward me. Not only do You put up with me, but You also pour out Your mercy on me and lead me out of confusion and distress."

His mercies are new every single morning because He is unfailing in His faithfulness to His sons and daughters: *"This I recall to my mind, therefore I have hope. Through the LORD's mercies we are not consumed, because **His compassions fail not**. They are new every morning; great is Your faithfulness"* (Lamentations 3:21–23 NKJV). This is our loving God; He displays His mercy generously, seeking us out so we won't miss it:

> *Who is a God like You, who pardons iniquity and passes over the rebellious act of the remnant of His possession? He does not retain His anger forever, because He delights in unchanging love. He will again have compassion on us; He will tread our iniquities under foot. Yes, You will cast all their sins into the depths of the sea. You will give truth to Jacob and unchanging love to Abraham, which You swore to our forefathers from the days of old.*   (Micah 7:18–20)

Aren't you grateful for His compassion? What would we do without it?

MERCIFUL AND PERSONAL

In spite of the lavish mercy that God extends toward each one of us, we must remember that not everyone recognizes it. Many people are blind to it, or they misinterpret it. I remember the vision that John Wimber had as he was driving home rejoicing about a successful healing he had just prayed for. He had been thinking about how most people, himself included, were actually afraid to pray for the sick because they thought God would not hear them. He realized most people have no idea that God's merciful, compassionate nature makes Him *want* to heal. Then Wimber had an open vision. It was so clear in his mind's eye that he felt he had to pull over to the side of the road to look at it more closely. He saw what appeared to be "a cloud bank superimposed across the sky":

> I had never seen a cloud bank like this one, so I pulled my car over to the side of the road to take a closer look. Then I realized it was not a cloud bank, it was a honeycomb with honey dripping out onto people below. The people were in a variety of postures. Some were reverent; they were weeping and holding their hands out to catch the honey and taste it, even inviting others to take some of their honey. Others acted irritated, wiping the honey off themselves, complaining about the mess.[10]

Wimber asked the Lord what this might be. "He said, 'It's my mercy, John. For some people it's a blessing, but for others it's a hindrance. There's plenty for everyone.'"[11] God's rich mercy is always falling on us, if we will only receive it with open hearts and hands.

Everything God does comes from the depths of His nature as a Father of compassion and mercy. He is *"the God of all comfort, who comforts us in all our troubles"* (2 Corinthians 1:3–4 NIV). He is *"a God of forgiveness, gracious and merciful, slow to become angry, and rich in unfailing love"* (Nehemiah 9:17 NLT). The Lord God Himself proclaimed His nature to Moses:

> The LORD passed in front of Moses, calling out, "Yahweh! The LORD! The God of compassion and mercy! I am slow to anger and filled with unfailing love and faithfulness." (Exodus 34:6 NLT)

The whole of the gospel is driven by God's compassion and mercy:

> He saved us, not on the basis of deeds which we have done in righteousness, but **according to His mercy**, by the washing of regeneration and renewing by the Holy Spirit, whom He poured out upon us richly through Jesus Christ our Savior, so that being justified by

10. John Wimber with Kevin Springer, *Power Healing* (San Francisco, CA: HarperCollins, 1987), 47–48.
11. Ibid.

His grace we would be made heirs according to the hope of eternal life. (Titus 3:5–7)

LOVE CAN MAKE A MIRACLE

My dear friend and mentor Mahesh Chavda described one of his early experiences in his book *Only Love Can Make a Miracle*. He was a young man living in Lubbock, Texas, and he had been asking the Lord for guidance regarding his decisions and actions. One day, he was roused from sleep with the deep conviction that he should go to work at the Lubbock State School, which cared for children who were profoundly disabled in their mental and physical capabilities. Up to that point, this kind of ministry had not been his "thing," but the conviction kept growing inside.

The Lord seemed to be saying, "I am a Father to the fatherless. And I am sending you as an ambassador of love to these little ones whom the world has forgotten." The Lord reminded him of this Scripture: *"Can a mother forget her nursing child? Can she feel no love for the child she has borne? But even if that were possible, I would not forget you!"* (Isaiah 49:15 NLT).

Mahesh followed through and applied for a job at the Lubbock State School, which was glad to have his services. He was assigned to the nonambulatory wards, where the children were confined to their beds and wheelchairs and could not walk. There, he would hold the children in turn in a rocking chair and just rock—and pray in the Spirit. God worked some healing miracles during that time, but the biggest miracle happened in Mahesh's own heart. When you allow the miracle of the compassion of Jesus to flow through you, you receive a deep draught of it yourself.

One little girl named Laura touched his heart in particular. Her mother had been using hard drugs during her pregnancy; as a result, Laura was born blind and severely retarded. Mahesh's duties took him from one nonambulatory ward to another, but he began to gravitate toward Laura's crib more and more, to the point that he would even go there after his working hours to hold her. She became quite precious to him.

After several weeks of rocking little Laura and praying over her, Mahesh happened to enter her ward during the daylight hours. As he approached her crib, she turned toward him and held up her arms in his direction. A number of staff members were nearby, and they were amazed. "Did you see that? Laura has never done that before," they said. The little blind baby had never before showed any response to anyone, not even after being touched. How did she know he was there? Was she beginning to regain her sight? How deeply she must have felt his love.

Mahesh had not been praying for healing. He had simply been holding each child in turn, praying that the Lord would somehow enable those children to experience His love through his actions. He was as surprised as anyone when love alone began to effect physical healings. He wrapped up the story like this:

> Now I was learning that the power of God was to be found in the love of God. When the Lord sent me to the State School, he did not say, "I am sending you as my ambassador of power or of miracles." He said, "I am sending you as my ambassador of love." That was the way I saw myself and that was the way I prayed for the children: that the Lord would make His love real to them. The healings came almost as a by-product. I learned that only love can make a miracle.[12]

God opened Mahesh's heart with compassion so that He could work freely through him in a hopeless place.

In a similar way, the Spirit of God moved in the heart of the father of the prodigal son in Jesus's story from Luke 15. Thus, when the destitute and rebellious son came trudging toward home, *"while he was still a long way off, his father saw him and was filled with compassion for him;*

---

12. Mahesh Chavda, *Only Love Can Make a Miracle* (Ann Arbor, MI: Servant Publications, 1990), 72–73.

he ran to his son, threw his arms around him and kissed him" (Luke 15:20 NIV). His heart overflowed with compassion and love for the son who had repudiated that love.

That's how it works. When the Father's compassion wells up in your heart, you act accordingly—and the impossible becomes possible! It can happen everywhere, from hospital bedsides to crime scenes.

Crime scenes? Yes, that could describe the setting of the parable of the good Samaritan:

> *Jesus replied and said, "A man was going down from Jerusalem to Jericho, and fell among robbers, and they stripped him and beat him, and went away leaving him half dead.... But a Samaritan, who was on a journey, came upon him; and when he saw him, he felt compassion, and came to him and bandaged up his wounds, pouring oil and wine on them; and he put him on his own beast, and brought him to an inn and took care of him.*   (Luke 10:30, 33–34)

The Good Samaritan's compassion-filled heart gave him the incentive to act on behalf of the stranger on the road, who had survived despite being beaten and robbed and left for dead.

I pray that you and I would learn to receive God's loving compassion and be quick to pass it on in ways that truly make a difference. Now let's look at one more distinction in this Feeler dimension as it pertains to the act of intervention.

WHEN THE FATHER'S COMPASSION WELLS UP IN YOUR HEART, YOU ACT ACCORDINGLY—AND THE IMPOSSIBLE BECOMES POSSIBLE!

PRIESTLY INTERVENTION

We are called to be priests of God in the world around us, ministering in whatever ways the Lord sees fit to use us. The writer of the letter to the Hebrews explains:

> *Every high priest is a man chosen to represent other people in their dealings with God. He presents their gifts to God and offers sacrifices for their sins. And he is able to deal gently with ignorant and wayward people because he himself is subject to the same weaknesses. That is why he must offer sacrifices for his own sins as well as theirs. And no one can become a high priest simply because he wants such an honor. He must be called by God for this work, just as Aaron was.* (Hebrews 5:1–4 NLT)

The primary reason it should be easy for us to step into a priestly role in our interactions and ministry is because we ourselves are subject to the same human weaknesses as anyone else. The trials I have gone through in recent years have put me in touch with the human condition I refer to as "the fragility of man." Knowing that we ourselves are made of the same stuff as the next person should make us much more patient with others and help us live more compassionate lives. This knowledge has produced in me a greater cry of "Lord, have mercy!"

SENSITIVITY TO THE NEEDS OF OTHERS

When God points out to us someone for whom we feel His love rising up inside us, we know it is time to reach out with a Spirit-filled heart of compassion and help that person. As Heidi Baker of Iris Ministries has so beautifully modeled for so many of us, we must learn to "stop for the one."

You and I are God's priests. *"You shall be named the priests of the* LORD, *they shall call you the servants of our God"* (Isaiah 61:6 NKJV). We are ministers in the name of the Lord. We have the same mission as the Lord Jesus Himself:

The Spirit of the Lord GOD *is upon Me, because the* LORD *has anointed Me to preach good tidings to the poor; He has sent Me to heal the brokenhearted, to proclaim liberty to the captives, and the opening of the prison to those who are bound; to proclaim the acceptable year of the* LORD, *and the day of vengeance of our God; to comfort all who mourn, to console those who mourn in Zion, to give them beauty for ashes, the oil of joy for mourning, the garment of praise for the spirit of heaviness; that they may be called trees of righteousness, the planting of the* LORD, *that He may be glorified.*

(Isaiah 61:1–3 NKJV; see also Luke 4:18–19)

KNOWING THAT WE OURSELVES ARE MADE OF THE SAME STUFF AS THE NEXT PERSON SHOULD MAKE US MUCH MORE PATIENT WITH OTHERS AND HELP US LIVE MORE COMPASSIONATE LIVES.

The results of our compassionate outreach are truly glorious, as the rest of Isaiah 61 attests.

Who knows? God's compassion rising up in your heart may mean that you find yourself doing what a young man in Nashville did not long ago: After befriending a homeless man on the streets, he was invited "home" to see the man's tent in the forest encampment outside the city. There were a number of others there. Like Jesus, this young man began to reach out to them, simply touching them on the forehead—whereupon some of them actually got healed right on the spot! His act of stopping for one led to an entire community of homeless people encountering the love of God. That is a testimony to the inherent power of the compassionate love of Christ.

Quite simply, compassion makes all the difference. As we go about our daily lives demonstrating what we have been given, we *"dispense true justice and practice kindness and compassion each to his brother"* (Zechariah 7:9). This means that we *"do not oppress the widow or the orphan, the stranger or the poor; and [we] do not devise evil in [our] hearts against one another"* (verse 10).

As I finalized this chapter, four EF4 tornadoes ripped through my hometown of Nashville, Tennessee. Much of the city is now in ruins. One moment, we were known around the world as the place to move for opportunity and entrepreneurship. Now, our narrative has temporarily been altered. God Encounters Ministries, among many other ministries, has been raising emergency relief funds and sending teams to serve, and bring hope to, those who are suffering the desolation of this natural disaster.

Putting many pending deadlines on pause, I went to look at the damage, to take it in, and to pray. I found myself in a district where the poor live, where the people have no insurance, no electricity, no food, and now no homes. Many were touched by the loss of life. As I sat there among the wreckage, the Holy Spirit spoke to my heart, saying, "I will have a revival of kindness where compassion takes action." That message gave me hope and renewed vision. I could see an army of helpers rising up who would "walk their talk" and let their hearts be moved with the very feelings of Christ Jesus.

At times like this, we need such "Feelers" as these to arise, people who can be led by the Spirit of God to let the world know that Somebody cares.

To close this pivotal chapter, let's take a line from Jude, the shortest book in the Bible: *"…have compassion, making a difference"* (Jude 1:22 KJV). That's my goal. Is it yours?

PRAYER OF A PASSIONATE HEART

Father, in Jesus's great name, I want to join with others and walk forth in the compassion of Jesus. I pray that I might feel what

Jesus felt and act as Jesus did. Please touch my senses with whatever moves Your heart. I volunteer to go wherever You send me. Here I am—all that You have made me and all that I hope to be as You continue Your work in my heart. For the sake of Your kingdom, pour Your compassion and love through me today and every day. Amen.

4

Sensitivity

*"Flowers appear on the earth; the season of singing has come,
the cooing of doves is heard in our land."*
—Song of Songs 2:12 (NIV)

The above verse from Song of Solomon[13] is rarely quoted except in relation to courtship or weddings; it is unusual to see it in a book like this. I chose this verse because I was looking for a Scripture that would signal tenderness and sensitivity, and I think this verse does that. Whether or not Song of Solomon was actually written by King Solomon, it contains many such poetic illustrations of tender feelings, yearning, compassion—in a word, *sensitivity*—and I appreciate its language for that reason.

The "cooing of doves" is heard in your land, right where you dwell, right now, today. The Holy Spirit is at work all around you, and your sensitivity to the Spirit plays a key part in your collaboration with Him to reach people for God. This is why it is so important to cultivate sensitivity to the Holy Spirit. You have decided to follow Him all the days

---

13. This biblical book is called "Song of Songs" in the *New International Version*.

of your life, and that means He is the Lord over even the smallest detail. From what you choose to wear to what you decide to eat, the Holy Spirit rejoices every time you make the right choices—ones that glorify God and reflect His goodness.

GROWING UP AS A SENSITIVE CHILD

Now we are about to get very up close and personal, at least from the perspective of the chair I have sat in for most of my life. Or, if we are going to be truly gut-level honest, all my life. At times, I was not certain if my sensitivity was a blessing or a curse. I did not feel like I had anyone with whom I could really share the depths of my inner being. As a child, I would pick up on things that nobody else seemed to be tuned in to. Have you ever felt that way? Overloaded and overwhelmed by feelings and sensations?

I often had to get out of the house and be alone. Frankly, at times, I was more comfortable being alone than I was being forced to hang out with the rough-and-tumble guys. I went on long walks along the railroad tracks in rural Cowgill, Missouri. I was at home there. I looked up at the clouds and talked to God, and I imagined that God talked back to me. There might have been a fine line between God being my imaginary escape mechanism and an actual, living reality. I don't know. I just know I talked to God, and He sure seemed to talk back.

Actually, I received the imprint of this conversational walk with God from one of my favorite hymns that we sang at church, "In the Garden":

And He walks with me, and He talks with me,

And He tells me I am His own,

And the joy we share as we tarry there,

None other has ever known.[14]

---

14. C. Austin Miles, "In the Garden" (1913), public domain, https://hymnary.org/text/i_come_to_the_garden_alone.

This song shaped my inner being, and to this day, I go back to it as a way of getting in touch with my root system.

On my walks, I would ask God questions like, "How are You today? Do You ever get lonely? Do You have friends? I would like to be Your friend, if that's okay with You." I would sometimes take off singing another old hymn, "What a Friend We Have in Jesus." Really? Yes, really.

My conversations were rather simple and profoundly complex at the same time. My subject matter was as broad as the universe. "How do You feel about this Cuban Missile Crisis? Is the world really coming to an end? Do You get afraid? I get afraid at night. I don't like being afraid. But I feel better now just letting You know about it. Okay?" And then I might go skipping along and singing another song. This time, it might be a Walt Disney tune like, "Let's go fly a kite / Up to the highest height…."

Singing always made me feel better, no matter the circumstances. To this day, singing has the same effect on me. It's what I've discovered to be my "sweet spot."

But I also almost always felt like the kid standing on the outside looking in. And yet, I was never sure I wanted in; based on what I could feel, hear, sense, and tell, I really did not want to be a part of what I felt was actually going on. Being on the outside looking in was kind of an awkward "safe place" to dwell. After all, I was more okay with what I could control. Such complexities for a kid to have been musing upon!

As a third grader at the Cowgill C-4 Elementary School, I had an active, curious mind, and I was so bored with my regular schoolwork that I also read all the books in the third-grade library, then sneaked over to the fourth-grade library and started reading through its limited selection of books. When I was done with that, I discovered a gold mine—the encyclopedias! I was really motivated to get my assignments done in record time so I could return to this treasure trove of information and read to my heart's content.

But baseball, football, and other standard pastimes of boys my age...I just did not connect with very well. It wasn't long before I had entered into those awkward years of asking myself, "How do I fit in? Do I fit in? Why am I like this?" Jeering, mocking, bullying...it all ran its course in my life and took a toll on me.

What is an extra-sensitive kid with a spiritual bent supposed to do? I just continued talking to God, walking with Jesus—my BBF—and singing. Yes, I just continued to talk to God and to listen to Him.

ARE YOU SENSITIVE?

When we say someone is "sensitive," what do we mean? In many cases, it means that we have to "walk on eggshells" around that person, right? You don't want to upset a sensitive person because of the potential fallout. In a positive sense, though, it can mean that the person's sensibilities are fine-tuned to pick up little environmental clues and subtle influences that help this individual navigate through life and relate to others.

Extra-sensitive people are "Feelers," and their antennae are always ready to receive signals. Without thinking about it, they will walk into a room and pick up the atmosphere, and their mood may be affected by it. Their sensitivity may present certain challenges. They may struggle with fearfulness, worry, or information overload, and they may be told to stop carrying the burdens of others so much. "Stop borrowing trouble; you're too sympathetic," people may urge them.

While Feelers may overthink and overreact to certain circumstances and situations, they also tend to have good intuition about what to do, or what to avoid doing. They may be quite creative, able to interpret their feelings via music, art, or writing. We will delve more deeply into these qualities in the next part of this chapter.

I'm describing a "born Feeler." When you add the Holy Spirit to the equation, you have a "born-again Feeler," a Spirit-filled Feeler. This person can sense God's direction as well as pick up information from the environment. A mature Feeler has learned how to be appropriately responsive to the needs of others as well as attentive to the often-subtle direction of the Holy Spirit, which is the most important part of being a Spirit-filled Feeler.

If you were born sensitive, your psyche may "bruise" easily. You may find that you are frequently offended and easily hurt. As you mature, your sensibilities need to be reeducated by the Holy Spirit so you can forgive personal affronts, stop nursing injured feelings, and allow your gift of sensitivity to be converted for the Master's use. Your sensitivity does not have to remain a weakness in your makeup. Instead, it can become your greatest strength.

> **WHILE FEELERS MAY OVERTHINK AND OVERREACT TO CERTAIN CIRCUMSTANCES AND SITUATIONS, THEY ALSO TEND TO HAVE GOOD INTUITION ABOUT WHAT TO DO, OR WHAT TO AVOID DOING.**

If you weren't born sensitive, you may become impatient with those who were, thinking they are too soft and way too emotional. Yet you can't judge them for their sensitivity when you recognize the fact that the Holy Spirit Himself is infinitely sensitive. God endows people with wide-ranging levels of sensitivity, and He wants to teach "Non-Feelers" how to read feelings better—even if, right now, you consider yourself to be about as sensitive as a fence post. Although you will never be a born Feeler, you can learn from God how to understand your human feelings better, how to empathize with others, and, above all, how to be sensitive to the still, small voice of His Spirit. (See 1 Kings 19:12 NKJV, KJV.)

In short, our Father God wants to help all of us, whether we consider ourselves "sensitive" or not, to grow and mature in our emotional responsiveness. He gave us our emotions, our feelings, our sensitivity, and our senses so we could better hear Him and follow His direction. Our feelings are part of our relationships on many levels, including our relationship with Him and our many relationships with our brothers and sisters in Christ and, of course, our natural family members. These feelings also contribute to our ability to reach out to strangers and form new relationships.

HIGHLY SENSITIVE PEOPLE

We can call a highly sensitive person an "HSP," a term devised by psychological researcher Dr. Elaine N. Aron and her husband, psychology professor Dr. Arthur Aron.[15] I consider myself an HSP and have found their research to be very helpful in understanding myself.

Before I expand on this topic, let me explain how I stumbled onto this research. Some years ago, I had a dear friend named David who was a born-again Jewish genius and was also very prophetically gifted. An incredibly innovative man, he was a leader in the marketplace. We traveled together in ministry across the U.S. and to other nations. My friend now dwells in heaven after an intense battle with cancer.

In a dream, David came to me with a book in his hand. He shoved it at my chest and said, "James, you've got to read this book. You really need to read this book. It will help you understand yourself and help you in training prophetic leaders." The book was none other than *The Highly Sensitive Person* by Elaine N. Aron. When I woke up, I remembered the dream, and although I did not recognize the title of the book, I immediately ordered it. You are now the beneficiary of this revelatory exchange.

Many HSPs can identify themselves by the following descriptions, summarized by the acronym DOES:

D is for Depth of processing. A foundational trait of an HSP is the tendency to process information more deeply than most other people. HSPs are often quite contemplative and function with good intuition.

---

15. See her website, hsperson.com. The HSP identifier was created by Elaine N. Aron, PhD, for her book *Psychotherapy and the Highly Sensitive Person* (New York: Routledge: Taylor & Francis Group, 2010). My description of the DOES acronym is taken from the revised version (2012) of this book.

O is for Overstimulation. HSPs tends to notice every little detail in any given situation. This can wear them out when complications, intensity, or confusion go on for too long; the stimulation is just too much. Non-HSP people will not notice such an overload of data in the first place.

E is for Emotional reactivity. E is also for Empathy. HSPs tend to react more to both positive and negative experiences. Not only do they experience stronger emotions, but brain-function studies show they also have higher levels of thinking and perceiving. HSPs not only know how someone else feels, but they actually feel that way themselves, to some extent.

S is for Sensing the subtle. HSPs are keenly aware of the little things that others tend to miss. This awareness of subtleties can prove useful when it comes to appreciating the simple pleasures of life or strategizing a response based on an awareness of the nonverbal cues others convey about their mood or their trustworthiness. However, it can also lead to sensory overload.

HOW THIS WORKS WITH ME

Besides identifying as an HSP, on other types of personality assessments, I see myself as an introvert, or a "high contemplator."[16] I think and feel intensely. I process things deeply and am affected emotionally (and even physically) by much of what goes on around me—including the unseen spiritual realm of angels and demons. It can be quite tiring to be highly sensitive, and sometimes I must withdraw from people to "recharge."

Many personality inventory tests differentiate between "introverts" and "extroverts." What is interesting is that I tend to be an "I," and then I become an "E." I am an introvert by nature, but I am an extrovert

16. I recently became certified as a Life Languages communications coach. The Life Languages system defines seven distinct forms of communication that everyone uses with different levels of fluency and preference. They call these seven modes of communication Responder, Shaper, Influencer, Mover, Producer, Doer, and Contemplator. My top three "languages" are Shaper, Responder, and Contemplator, which indicate a high capacity for thinking and feeling.

by vocational function. Therefore, I require periods of "alone time" to recharge so that I can function with grace, energy, and vivaciousness while ministering in public. Now, back to the HSP dynamics.

At times, I pick up on other people's suffering or need. For example, I was in a restaurant, and when a server walked by, I sensed the woman's emotional pain, as well as a physical pain in her shoulder. I started to feel unreasonably sad, and my own shoulder suddenly began throbbing with pain. My senses perked up on this individual amid a crowd. Then, as the Holy Spirit led me, I reached out to her with an encouraging word and an invitation to receive prayer for healing. This is how, in terms of spiritual gifting, the "E" of DOES—Emotional reactivity or Empathy—spills over into words of knowledge and then into gifts of healings. It was so great! Yes, the Holy Spirit touched her right then and there, and the pain immediately left her (and me as well!).

It has helped me enormously to read about HSPs and to integrate the insights of Dr. Aron with other self-assessment paradigms. Now I understand myself better, and I can share my knowledge with others so they can understand themselves and others better. I work within a context of an integrated healing, counseling, and prophetic model. When we are internally whole, we externally integrate better.

What wonderful news that having this set of qualities does not make Feelers deficient, weak, or substandard. We all have weaknesses, but knowing how sensitivity can be a strength helps us in our active pursuit of godliness. Our understanding always needs a divine touch, or we will wallow in our sensitivities and risk becoming "high-maintenance" individuals with few friends.

HSPs (and other types) need to submit their understandings and insights to God, pray over them, and learn from Him what do to with them. Our self-knowledge always needs to be fine-tuned and kept under the lordship of Jesus.

Remember the prophet Daniel? The Bible tells us that he was well-taught in literature and all the knowledge of the Babylonians. In addition, God gave him supernatural insight. (See Daniel 1:3–4, 6, 17.)

God's divine touch made all the difference for Daniel and his three friends—and it makes all the difference for us. We should know how we "tick," but we must also invite God's Holy Spirit to take charge of our every strength and every weakness so that He can rule over our particular set of sensitivities. Then we will have the joy of watching what God does through us.

Know this: God's grace is perfected in our weaknesses! (See 2 Corinthians 12:9.) And also know that God opposes the proud but gives grace to the humble. (See James 4:6.)

> *WE ALL HAVE WEAKNESSES, BUT KNOWING HOW SENSITIVITY CAN BE A STRENGTH HELPS US IN OUR ACTIVE PURSUIT OF GODLINESS.*

SENSITIVITY TO THE HOLY SPIRIT

Are HSPs more sensitive to the Holy Spirit? To answer that question, we must first ask, what is the Holy Spirit like, anyway?

In the Bible, the Holy Spirit is known by many names, and each name portrays an aspect of His nature. Here are several of His titles:

+ Comforter (see John 14:26 KJV)

+ Eternal Spirit (see Hebrews 9:14)

+ Spirit of Promise (see Ephesians 1:13)

+ Promise of the Father (see Luke 24:49)

+ Spirit of Glory (see 1 Peter 4:14)

+ Spirit of Prophecy (see Revelation 19:10)

+ Spirit of Christ (see 1 Peter 1:11)

I could preach a sermon about any one of these aspects of the nature of the Holy Spirit. I have written about them at length in books such as *Passionate Pursuit: Getting to Know God and His Word* and *Living a Supernatural Life: The Secret to Experiencing a Life of Miracles.* His names and characteristics become especially meaningful to us as we experience Him at different times in our lives. Right now, because He has been looking after me so consistently, I am most lifted up when I think of His faithfulness as the Promise of the Father.

The Holy Spirit is an invisible Spirit, which is why the Scriptures tend to use metaphors, or word pictures, to describe Him and what He does. These symbols reveal the nature of the Spirit of God and teach us how to relate to Him. Scripture compares the Spirit to a variety of entities that are quite familiar to us, such as the following:

- A dove (see Matthew 3:16; Luke 3:22; John 1:32)
- Water (see John 4:14)
- Rain (see Joel 2:23)
- Holy anointing oil (see Psalm 89:20)
- Wind (see John 3:8; Acts 2:2)
- Flames of fire (see Isaiah 4:4; Luke 3:16; Acts 2:3)

We say that the Holy Spirit is "like" all of these entities because we are trying to describe His characteristic personality traits. He is not, in fact, any of these things. Not every dove is the Spirit. And flames sometimes remind us of evil. To differentiate and understand, we have to experience for ourselves the invisible realities of the metaphors.

Most important, the Holy Spirit is a *Person*. And, as people often say, "The Holy Spirit is a Gentleman." He will not force His way into your life. He will rarely announce His presence in a blatant manner. For this reason, it can be easy to miss Him. Now, let's also be clear that while part of His nature is to be gentle, He is also referred to as tongues of fire and a rushing wind. So, I have discovered that the Holy Spirit is equally the Divine Disrupter. He is a bold Gentleman! (I just had to get that in there!)

I find it instinctive to turn to Him, after so many years of seeking God. But many people do not feel or see it that way. They ignore Him, or they may even ridicule Him. To some, He is a doctrine and not a living, moving Being. Others (this applies to believers only) take Him for granted. To them, the members of the Trinity—the Father, His Son Jesus, and the Holy Spirit—become ordinary, even boring, background figures in their lives.

Even John the Baptist had this problem to a degree. John was, in actual fact, the forerunner of the Messiah, the fulfillment of the prophecy of Isaiah 40:3, expressed in John 1:23 as follows: *"The voice of one crying in the wilderness: 'Make straight the way of the Lord'"* (NKJV). But John was also Jesus's cousin, only about six months older than He. The two may have played together as children. Did overfamiliarity hinder John's perception of Jesus as the Messiah? I have wondered about that when reading his reaction to reports of Jesus's ministry—for example, in the account from Matthew 11.

If that were the case, we do know that John overcame the obstacle of familiarity and was able, by dependency on the Holy Spirit, to identify and proclaim that Jesus was indeed the Lamb of God, the one and only Son of God. (See John 1:29.) For a cousin to receive that level of revelation, it would have required sensitivity to and from the Holy Spirit.

Now, back to the original question. Are HSPs more sensitive to the Holy Spirit than other people? Anyone can be as close to God as they desire to be. We know that the Holy Spirit's sensitive nature is the same no matter the condition of a person, and we know that God's grace is perfected in our weaknesses. So, I believe that our natural sensitivity can certainly be a useful tool for discerning the ministry and movement of the Holy Spirit. But I do not believe that a lack of natural sensitivity necessarily limits a person's supernatural capacity to move in the gifts of the Holy Spirit.

HOLY SPIRIT, YOU ARE WELCOME

Scripture warns us against grieving the ever-sensitive Holy Spirit: "*Do not grieve* [or insult] *the Holy Spirit of God*" (Ephesians 4:30). The idea of "grieving" the Spirit covers a lot of negatives. The Word says, "*Do not quench the Spirit*" (1 Thessalonians 5:19) and "Do not lie to the Spirit" (see Acts 5:3). Not only does the Bible make clear that we should not be ignorant of the Spirit of God (see 1 Corinthians 12:1), but— stern warning here—it tells us, "Do not blaspheme against the Holy Spirit" (see, for example, Matthew 12:31).

In glorious contrast, the Word also urges us to be eager to invite the Holy Spirit into our lives. However, this means more than inviting Him to be our holy Guest, because He owns the whole house! We must be quick to say, "Holy Spirit, You are welcome in my life. Help Yourself to anything. I give You complete liberty."

Just look at all these biblical invitations to submit and consent to the rulership of the Spirit of God:

+ Seek Him. (See Deuteronomy 4:29; Luke 12:31.)

+ Honor Him. (See 1 Samuel 2:30; 1 Corinthians 6:20.)

+ Give Him free rein in your life. (See Job 22:21; James 4:7.)

+ Be born of the Spirit. (See Ezekiel 36:25–27; John 3:5.)

+ Receive the Holy Spirit. (See John 20:22.)

+ Worship in the Spirit. (See John 4:24.)

+ Serve others in obedience to the Spirit. (See 1 Corinthians 12:7.)

+ Be baptized with the Holy Spirit. (See Matthew 3:11; Acts 11:16.)

+ Be continuously filled with the Spirit. (See John 14:16–17; Ephesians 5:18.)

+ Be led by the Spirit. (See Romans 8:14; Galatians 5:18.)

+ Pray in the Spirit. (See Ephesians 6:18; Jude 1:20.)

+ Hear the Spirit. (See John 8:47.)

+ Walk in the Spirit. (See Galatians 5:16; Ephesians 5:8.)

Such Scriptures are not addressed only to Feelers, of course, but you can see how our sensitivities come into play when we relate to the Holy Spirit. Where the Holy Spirit is concerned, entering into the Feeler realm should not be a rare experience reserved for only a special few—it is accessible for every believer who seeks His presence.

What if you were to seek Him more earnestly? What if you changed your assumptions and expected a little more heaven on earth when you prayed? Avoid the instability of walking by your feelings or emotions alone, and instead walk by spiritual sight, shining the light of the Word on your path. (See Psalm 119:105.) Put your heart into your search as you pray the Word.

> **WE MUST BE QUICK TO SAY, "HOLY SPIRIT, YOU ARE WELCOME IN MY LIFE. HELP YOURSELF TO ANYTHING. I GIVE YOU COMPLETE LIBERTY."**

Take time to discover what you can do to please the Lord. Paul wrote to the Ephesian church, *"Find out what pleases the Lord"* (Ephesians 5:10 NIV). It's an adventure you don't want to miss. No one automatically knows what pleases the Lord, but He will guide our search when we genuinely seek Him. We can learn to tune in with our senses and be open to His.

I remember when Michal Ann, my late wife, discovered more about her mother's interest in birdwatching. Her mother would go out into the woods or on a drive, taking a notebook and a little stool and her binoculars, and she would log every bird she saw. She learned to recognize them by the shadows they cast, their chirps, the colors and patterns of their feathers, their shapes and habits, and their flight patterns. That is more or less what I am talking about when I say, "Seek Him." Exercise your senses. Undertake your search with a sense of purpose.

Expect to feel, hear, and see the Spirit as He responds to your invitation. The Holy Spirit is the third person of the Godhead, and He has an exquisitely sensitive personality. He is not an "it." Seek Him out and learn to cultivate intimacy with Him; you will never regret the effort.

As we integrate the diverse dimensions of sensitivity into our lives, we can learn to be tender and sensitive, living from our hearts instead of responding only in a cerebral or compartmentalized way. With the Holy Spirit in control, we can be more caring toward others and better at communicating with people. For all our lives, we can continue to grow in our revelation about the nature of the Holy Spirit, embracing His sensitivity.

Remember, the depth of our hunger is the length of our reach to God. Hunger attracts the Holy Spirit of God!

PRAYER OF A PASSIONATE HEART

Father, because of Jesus and Your Spirit, I love You. I present myself to You and bring You my personality, my unique sensitivity level, and my weaknesses. May Your Holy Spirit descend and remain upon my life as He did with Jesus. Fill me. Shape me. Use me. Give me a heart of tenderness for Your kingdom's sake. Mold me to suit Your will and Your ways. You are the Potter, and I am the clay—fashion me to Your liking. I want to do only what is pleasing in Your sight, from this time forward. Amen and amen!

5

How to Respond to Feelings

"For all who are led by the Spirit of God are children of God."
—Romans 8:14 (NLT)

Before we start digging into the theme of this chapter, let's make sure we have a good foundation, a good root system, of the truth of God's Word in our hearts and minds. After all, unless we are grounded in biblical wisdom, we can't expect to respond properly to our emotional perceptions. Our feelings must be fully surrendered to the lordship of Christ and the truth of God's Word because they are nowhere near as reliable as the Word. It is all-important that we learn to interpret our feelings through the lens that the Word of God provides.

GROUNDED IN THE WORD

Do you love your Bible? Does your Bible speak to you? When you read the Scriptures or listen to them being read, do you savor the verses one by one? Do you embrace the messages of the stories? Do you saturate yourself in God's Word? No condemnation intended. Just a few questions to ponder as we begin this chapter on responding to our feelings.

Years ago, when I was part of the staff of what is now Metro Christian Fellowship with Mike Bickle, staff members did not have assigned offices; we simply used whatever office was open when we needed space. One day, I met with someone for a pastoral appointment in one of the upstairs offices, and I took with me my favorite Moody Bible, a *New American Standard Bible* translation. It had a brown leather cover, and I took it everywhere with me.

Well, wouldn't you know, by mistake, I left it in the office I had been occasionally using. I didn't miss it until much later that day. At that point, I couldn't remember where I'd put it down. It was missing for two or three weeks. Of course, I had other Bibles—of all sizes and covers and several different translations—but they weren't "my" Bible, the one I was most familiar with. I felt lost without it. This was the one with all the special notations in it and my personalized comments. It even had beloved scribbles and markings from my kids. None of my other Bibles had the same look or feel. In the others, I couldn't find what I wanted as quickly as I could in my good old brown leather Moody Bible.

Then, one day, I happened to go to an upstairs office at the church, and there I found it! It had been sitting there the whole time. I swept it up in my hands, held it to my heart, and ran out into the hallway, rejoicing. Bursting with happiness, I kept exclaiming as I ran down the hallway, "I found my friend! I found my friend!" I remember that encounter like it was yesterday. "I found my friend!"

A side story: Michal Ann never missed a day reading her Bible. On multiple occasions, she referred to her copy of *The Amplified Bible* as her most treasured possession. I was told an endearing story by her mother, Dorris, that I will attempt to pass on to you. One time, when Ann was a young girl, the rest of the family members were waiting in the sedan to go to town, but she was nowhere to be found. One of her three older brothers was sent to the house to go find his little sister.

There she was in her upstairs bedroom, quietly sitting on her bed, simply reading her Bible. She had been in her own little world, oblivious to the honking horn of the car and to everything else around her, so captured was she by the Word of God. You see, her Bible was her best friend too!

Yes, I loved the Word then, and I love it to this day. I read it constantly, and God speaks to me through it. It is safe to say I have grounded my life in the Word. I recommend you do the same—it's full of love and joy and good news!

Now, I realize that all this might come across like pie-in-the-sky living, as though I daily walk on "Easy Street." Far from it! I have had hard days. I have walked through some really rough times and rather deep valleys. In recent years, I've struggled day and night with intense sciatic nerve pain from a failed back surgery, and I am often fighting to keep my "cookies together." Okay? But that is all the more reason why I must turn to the Word to God to make sure my mind and emotions are renewed daily and I am responding properly and not overreacting.

GROUNDED IN THE CHURCH

To be well-grounded requires being well-planted in the first place—being firmly rooted and growing steadily. The interpretation of Jesus's parable of the sower, a teaching we looked at earlier in the version from the gospel of Matthew, applies to us:

> Now the parable is this: the seed is the word of God. Those beside the road are those who have heard; then the devil comes and takes away the word from their heart, so that they will not believe and be saved. Those on the rocky soil are those who, when they hear, receive the word with joy; and these have no firm root; they believe for a while, and in time of temptation fall away. The seed which fell among the thorns, these are the ones who have heard, and as they go on their way they are choked with worries and riches and pleasures of this life, and bring no fruit to maturity. (Luke 8:11–14)

The best soil in which to grow is found in the body of Christ, of course. As you participate regularly in corporate worship and fellowship with your brothers and sisters in Christ, and as you listen to sound teaching about God's truth, you will flourish. That is the way to find your special place in the body, and that is how you learn to work together with others under the leadership of the Spirit.

Even when hard times threaten to overwhelm you, you are much more likely to flourish if you are part of a local church and not off on your own somewhere. The writer of the book of Hebrews urges all of us to *"consider how we may spur one another on toward love and good deeds, not giving up meeting together, as some are in the habit of doing, but encouraging one another—and all the more as you see the Day approaching"* (Hebrews 10:24–25 NIV).

Sad to say, one of the greatest weaknesses in the body of Christ today is the high number of people who claim to be so exceptionally "spiritual" that they conduct their lives aloof from others. Not only aren't they well-grounded in the written Word of God, but they also haven't submitted their lives to a body of believers. They move from place to place, seeking a spiritual home, of sorts; but as soon as they discover something they don't like about a place, they start roaming again. Their independent lifestyle makes them miss out on the course corrections and personal growth that come from being immersed in the Word alongside others who love its Author, and they also miss out on the encouragement God could have given them as they walked through life together with fellow believers.

EVEN WHEN HARD TIMES THREATEN TO OVERWHELM YOU, YOU ARE MUCH MORE LIKELY TO FLOURISH IF YOU ARE PART OF A LOCAL CHURCH AND NOT OFF ON YOUR OWN SOMEWHERE.

They may think of themselves as pioneers, forerunners, or ground-breakers, but they will not grow into the fullness of life in Christ if they remain isolated from others. Until the storms of life hit them, they don't realize how very vulnerable they are, like stray cornstalks that spring up outside the boundaries of the farmer's field. Self-regulating to a fault, they don't want to entrust their welfare to others, and they assume they can discover all the resources of the kingdom on their own.

Even as my ministry has taken me many places over the years, I have always made sure to become part of a local body of believers. I highly value church participation and membership, and I make it a point to be more than just a Sunday-morning attendee. I have been part of about seven churches in my lifetime, and each of these bodies of believers has helped to keep me well-grounded. No church anywhere on earth is perfect, but that is not the point. If I had decided to join the church that met all of my perceived needs without a glitch and matched each and every one of my personal convictions, I'd still be looking for it!

Oh, by the way, I do believe there are multiple valid expressions of the *ecclesia*—the church, the called-out ones. The issue is that the new wine needs a new wineskin. (See, for example, Matthew 9:17.) They go together. The believer both receives from and contributes to a local body of believers to which they are committed. We need each other!

Living out your faith in the context of the local Christian body can also teach you about historical precedents. From your perspective as a believer, everything may seem new and fresh and exciting. There is nothing inherently wrong with that, yet your viewpoint is always influenced by the culture around you and by your background. You will never grow very much without learning wisdom lessons from those who have gone before you.

Walking alongside other believers means that you will never have to "reinvent the wheel" when it comes to spiritual things. In fact, you will probably get seriously off track if you try to figure everything out on your own, even if you think you are good at it. If you value the church, you will not have to learn everything the hard way because others have paved the way ahead for you.

Many saints who are now with the Lord have left a written record of the lessons they learned. Those who are still alive can be heard in the context of the local and the global body of Christ. Believers are foolish to neglect such wisdom.

So, my question is, are you rooted like a well-planted tree, like the one described in the very first psalm?

Blessed is the one who does not walk in step with the wicked or stand in the way that sinners take or sit in the company of mockers, but whose delight is in the law of the LORD, and who meditates on his law day and night. That person is like a tree planted by streams of water, which yields its fruit in season and whose leaf does not wither—whatever they do prospers. Not so the wicked! They are like chaff that the wind blows away. Therefore the wicked will not stand in the judgment, nor sinners in the assembly of the righteous. For the LORD watches over the way of the righteous, but the way of the wicked leads to destruction. (Psalm 1:1–6 NIV)

What kind of tree are you? Your health, the degree of your spiritual growth, and the fruit you bear are all dependent on the quality of your root system and the care you give to it.

LED BY THE SPIRIT

After you have established a strong root system, you can explore what it means to be led by the Spirit. The Holy Spirit is not "out there" somewhere, hiding and invisible, but rather is dwelling within your own spirit, as well as within the spirit of each believer who has ever lived. *"The one who joins himself to the Lord is one spirit with Him"* (1 Corinthians 6:17). Paul considered it his calling to unveil this mystery:

I now rejoice in my sufferings for you, and fill up in my flesh what is lacking in the afflictions of Christ, for the sake of His body, which is the church, of which I became a minister according to the stewardship from God which was given to me for you, to fulfill the word of God, the mystery which has been hidden from ages and from generations, but now has been revealed to His saints. To them God willed to make known what are the riches of the glory of this mystery among the Gentiles: which is Christ in you, the hope of glory.

(Colossians 1:24–27 NKJV)

The glory of Jesus Christ has been and continues to be revealed to us, thanks to the Holy Spirit. Now we can preach the Word with power and show the winsome love of Christ, making new disciples for Him and with Him. Jesus said, *"Ye shall receive power, after that the Holy Ghost is come upon you: and ye shall be witnesses unto me both in Jerusalem, and in all Judaea, and in Samaria, and unto the uttermost part of the earth"* (Acts 1:8 KJV).

Being indwelt by the Spirit occurs through our faith by our purposeful invitation and consent. Many believers are little aware of the Spirit's presence; they don't feel anything. But, for Feelers, being filled with the Spirit is more likely to be accompanied by tangible manifestations. This certainly helps them become conscious of the Holy Spirit, and may assist them as they learn to operate in tune with the Spirit.

We grow up accustomed to being led by our soul—often defined as the mind, the will, and the emotions—and doing things on our own. But once we meet our Savior and give our lives to Him, we must start to learn how to walk all over again and how to respond to the Spirit of Christ dwelling in union with our spirit. We have been granted the great privilege of learning to function effectively in a wonderfully dynamic relationship. As Scripture says:

These are the ones who follow the Lamb wherever He goes.

(Revelation 14:4)

If you are led by the Spirit, you are not under the Law.

(Galatians 5:18)

"I will put My Spirit within you and you will come to life, and I will place you on your own land. Then you will know that I, the LORD, have spoken and done it," declares the LORD. (Ezekiel 37:14)

Consider, for a moment, the following questions:

+ Do you follow the Lamb wherever He goes?

+ Are you well-grounded so you can grow like a tree planted by streams of water, bearing good fruit?

+ Are you living so much in union with Jesus that your decisions and actions are no longer conditioned by circumstances or tainted with personal ambition?

+ Are you learning how to test the spirits and resolving to follow after God's Holy Spirit wherever He leads you?

It is my wholehearted desire to abide with Him like that, and I trust it is yours as well.

SPIRIT, SOUL, AND BODY

Humans are brilliantly complex beings, created as we are in the image of God. The psalmist exulted in his knowledge of this truth: *"I am fearfully and wonderfully made"* (Psalm 139:14). But if we remain unredeemed, the capacity of our wonderful complexity will be quite limited. Only after we have surrendered ourselves to the Lord Jesus can we begin to fully appreciate and operate out of our individual God-designed selves. The apostle Paul prayed this fervent prayer for the believers under his care: *"May God himself, the God of peace, sanctify you through and through. May your whole **spirit, soul and body** be kept blameless at the coming of our Lord Jesus Christ"* (1 Thessalonians 5:23 NIV).

"Spirit, soul and body." You *are* a spirit, you *have* a soul, and you *live* in a physical body. Compared with your spirit, your soul is not "bad," and neither is your body. No, the spirit, soul, and body work together at all times. It takes all three components, united and functioning as one, to represent the image of the triune God.

It is your spirit that makes you alive. You are going to live forever, either in heaven or in hell. Spirits are eternal. Your spirit is invisible, but it dwells in a physical body, which limits and directs its expression of life.

Your soul deserves some extra attention, especially in a book that is all about the importance of senses and feelings. What is the soul, anyway? The human soul, as indicated earlier, is often described as being composed of the mind, the will, and the emotions. The component parts are usually stated in that order, with emotions "bringing up the rear," somehow not being given as much attention in Christian circles as the mind and the will. Because this book has been written to help you better understand how your emotions come into play, it is important to consider how they contribute to the way your soul functions.

SPIRIT, SOUL, AND BODY WORK TOGETHER AT ALL TIMES. IT TAKES ALL THREE COMPONENTS, UNITED AND FUNCTIONING AS ONE, TO REPRESENT THE IMAGE OF THE TRIUNE GOD.

What does our soul do for us? I have received some fresh understandings in recent years, including the realization that our soul is, all at the same time, a *receiver*, a *translator*, and an *interpreter*. You cannot detect and understand a radio signal unless you have a radio receiver. Likewise, without your soul, you cannot begin to understand the information that your senses take in. The human soul is the receiver of information and revelation from multiple sources, receiving input by listening and watching attentively through all of its sensory "gateways," including what I like to term the sixth sense, the gateway of knowing.

However, at first, the information the soul receives is just dumped, not sorted. This fact is really necessary to grasp, especially for us Feeler types. We are inundated with information on a daily basis: news, opinions, images, cultural and philosophical systems. More than that, we are pummeled from within and without by our fleshly desires and by spiritual atmospheres. Data, both sought and unsolicited, is being transmitted to our souls all the time; some comes from the powers of darkness, some comes from our own minds, and some comes from the Holy Spirit. How can we determine what we should keep and what we should discard? How can we figure out what to do with all of it?

This is where our soul as *translator* and *interpreter* comes in. Our soul translates the impulses into "readable" signals, interpreting them in accordance with our existing filters, prejudices, and background. Some of this information further imprints our soul "filter" as it is received, translated, and interpreted. Our mind and emotions react to the information.

During all our waking hours, our soul is forwarding notices, alerts, sensations, warnings, and a whole range of other reactions and responses. Some input gets only brief attention, while other input is ignored entirely and passed over. The rest is retained in some form, either becoming memories (many as background memories, even unconscious ones) or fodder for formulating active decisions, which we make using our mind and will.

Our soul is the storage place for memories, good and bad, from all of our life experiences. Our memories surface (or not) depending on what triggers get pushed. As you may be aware, your dream life is often a reflection of the condition of your soul; dreams employ your stored memories as tools of communication.

It will not come as a surprise to you that memories carry emotions. When a memory surfaces, it may well be accompanied by a flood of emotions. Some of these emotions may be quite strong and potentially damaging. This is why, in Christian circles, we sometimes talk about the "healing of memories." While we recognize that God does not want to erase our memories, we have developed techniques for listening to our memories so that, by the power of choosing forgiveness and applying the healing blood of Jesus to old wounds, we can stop the sting and prevent any further damage. Thus, while the memory remains, the emotional pain is lessened and eventually can be released and removed.

Then we move into the next brilliant stage of our process—that of renewal.

RENEWING OUR SOUL

One of the great benefits of our new life in Christ is that we get to refresh and renew our soul. This is scriptural. Two passages that address soul renewal directly are found in Paul's epistles to the Romans and to the Corinthians:

Do not conform to the pattern of this world, but be transformed by the renewing of your mind. Then you will be able to test and approve what God's will is—his good, pleasing and perfect will.

(Romans 12:2 NIV)

The weapons we fight with are not the weapons of the world. On the contrary, they have divine power to demolish strongholds. We demolish arguments and every pretension that sets itself up against the knowledge of God, and we take captive every thought to make it obedient to Christ.   (2 Corinthians 10:4–5 NIV)

Enemies of your soul, both external and internal, are out to infect you with lies. You have to know how to defend yourself, and how to recover from assaults.[17]

In brief, when you know how to identify ungodly beliefs, you can turn around and adopt godly beliefs in their place. It is not a complicated process, but it can be difficult because, at times, it is easy to become confused about what is ungodly. The Holy Spirit will help you because He dwells in your heart, and you are a co-laborer with Him. He will shine His light on ungodly beliefs (not too many at one time, so as not to overwhelm you) to help you see how they fail to line up with the Word of God. You may have developed some persistent thought patterns that have established strongholds in your mind. But even lifelong strongholds are not too strong to withstand the divinely powerful weapons

---

17. My book *Deliverance from Darkness* (Grand Rapids, MI: Chosen Books, 2010) goes into great detail about the weapons of our spiritual warfare.

of Christ Jesus, with which you can dismantle any ungodly stronghold. Because, again, *"the weapons we fight with are not the weapons of the world. On the contrary, they have divine power to demolish strongholds."*

Repentance and forgiveness will always be first steps. As you open your heart to God's light, and as the truth of the situation becomes apparent, be quick to take responsibility for any ungodly beliefs you may have been harboring. Do whatever He shows you, and ask Him for the courage and fortitude you need to carry it out.

Then you can move into newness. You can adopt godly beliefs, which He will show you when you seek Him. James writes, *"Therefore lay aside all filthiness and overflow of wickedness, and receive with meekness the implanted word, which is able to save your souls. But be doers of the word, and not hearers only, deceiving yourselves"* (James 1:21–22 NKJV). Amazingly, the divine Word can effect permanent changes in your soul.

The choice is yours to make, and yours alone. Without giving intentional, even aggressive, attention to the healing of your soul, you will waste much time and effort pulling yourself out of the ditch on your journey of life. If you attend to your soul's welfare, you can move out into the dimension of sanctified thoughts, feelings, and emotions and be responsive to the Holy Spirit rather than reacting to everything through the filter of your unhealed soul.

A simple verse from 3 John clearly portrays the will of God for our lives: *"Beloved, I pray that you may prosper in all things and be in health, just as your soul prospers"* (3 John 1:2 NKJV).

YIELD THE RIGHT-OF-WAY

Give God total control of your life—total jurisdiction over its management. Don't knowingly retain any rights, and be quick to surrender anew if you revert to controlling some aspect of your life. Turn over your preconceived prejudices and your soul wounds so you can freely go wherever He directs you.

As you know, God's Spirit is like the wind: *"The wind blows where it wishes, and you hear the sound of it, but cannot tell where it comes from and where it goes. So is everyone who is born of the Spirit*" (John 3:8 NKJV). No one can see the wind, although we can observe its effects. We can hear and feel the wind, but we can't determine its direction. With practice, we can learn to sail by wind power. Without dictating to the Holy Spirit what He should do in us or how He should use us, we can nevertheless be ready and willing to cooperate with Him, even when we realize that His intention is to excavate and rebuild our souls.

Again, the choice is ours to make. We can react either out of unhealthy and unsanctified emotions, or we can respond from the fruit of the Spirit—love, joy, peace, patience, kindness, goodness, faithfulness, gentleness, and self-control. (See Galatians 5:22–23.) When we react out of unhealed places in our souls, we find ourselves separated from the refreshment of the Holy Spirit. Healthier responses happen when our minds, wills, and emotions have been transformed by the Word and Spirit of God.

God's will for you is always perfect and good. He will help you respond to His Spirit with the right combination of energy and patience. He will see to it that, like a well-rooted and healthy tree, your life bears good fruit for His kingdom.

So how do you, as a sensitive member of the body of Christ, appropriately respond to your feelings and emotions? You do it by being renewed by God's Word one day at a time. This will enable you to say yes to Him every day, with joy. Then you will be a clean, more whole candidate to receive, sense, and feel the Holy Spirit's impulses and know how to properly respond. It is actually quite an exciting journey!

GOD WILL SEE TO IT THAT, LIKE A WELL-ROOTED AND HEALTHY TREE, YOUR LIFE BEARS GOOD FRUIT FOR HIS KINGDOM.

PRAYER OF A PASSIONATE HEART

Father, You know I want to learn how to properly respond to Your work in my soul. I want to respond rather than react out of my existing worldview, which includes various false ideas and perceptions. Guide me into healing and sanctification. Identify my wounds, many of which I have fostered and excused. Move in on the ungodly misbeliefs that have chained my soul in captivity. Teach me how to identify them, and help me to replace them with new and godly beliefs based on Your Word. Anoint my neglected Feeler realm as it comes into alignment with Your Word, will, and ways. I surrender myself to being led by Your Holy Spirit from this time forward. I pray all this in the mighty name of Jesus. Amen.

6

The Fruit of the Spirit

"The fruit of the Spirit is love, joy, peace, patience, kindness,
goodness, faithfulness, gentleness, self-control;
against such things there is no law."
—Galatians 5:22–23

I love fruit. Don't you? For just a moment, let's take a little stroll together down an imaginary lane and look at some fruit trees. Oh, the lush apples. There are so many colors and varieties to choose from: red, green, yellow…. Wow, look at those Georgia peaches! And the apricots make my mouth water. Cherries…I love cherry pie! And then there are the pears…I might just start singing a Christmas song right now. Oranges, grapefruit, limes…and don't forget the lemons. The lemon tree is oh so pretty.

Over to the side, there is a garden filled with—guess what—strawberries! And there is a field full of more berries: blueberries, blackberries, boysenberries, raspberries, gooseberries, and every other berry you can think of. Not to mention the vineyards overflowing with delightful grapes—red, purple, and green. There has to be some rhubarb around here somewhere. There might be a pumpkin patch nearby too.

Every fruit, in the natural, is unique. Every fruit has a distinct look, feel, taste, and even purpose. God, in His majesty, also has a variety of fruit of the Spirit, each with a distinct look, feel, and purpose. For the sensitized Feeler, understanding and walking in the fruit of the Spirit is paramount!

The nine kinds of fruit mentioned in Galatians 5:22–23—love, joy, peace, patience, kindness, goodness, faithfulness, gentleness, and self-control—are summed up in the very first fruit on the list, *love*. "God *is love*" (1 John 4:8, 16), and when His Spirit is allowed full liberty in a person's soul, the fruit of love begins to grow and mature.

However, before we ever started bearing the good fruit of the Spirit, most of us probably expended a great deal of energy bearing bad fruit. In fact, bad fruit will always be the "default" characteristic of any unredeemed human life.

Only Jesus can reclaim a life so that it bears good fruit, and He said, *"Either make the tree good and its fruit good, or else make the tree bad and its fruit bad; for a tree is known by its fruit"* (Matthew 12:33 NKJV). Jesus volunteered to do what was necessary to make it possible for even the sickest tree (man or woman) in the world to recover and flourish and be fruitful. But we must choose to follow Him and keep obeying Him on a daily basis.

WHAT DOES BAD FRUIT LOOK LIKE?

We can blame the desires of our flesh—our bodies—for producing the impulses that give rise to bad fruit. Scripture makes this clear:

> *Now the **deeds of the flesh** are evident, which are: immorality, impurity, sensuality, idolatry, sorcery, enmities, strife, jealousy, outbursts of anger, disputes, dissensions, factions, envying, drunkenness, carousing, and things like these, of which I forewarn you....*
> (Galatians 5:19–21)

Paul, who composed this list, went on to add, *"I have forewarned you, that those who practice such things will not inherit the kingdom of God"* (verse 21).

Of course, this is only a representative list. The deeds of the flesh multiply like weeds wherever human nature prevails. If you are unable to name a few of your own deeds of the flesh, just pause for a couple of minutes and recall how grumpy you were to a family member this morning or how selfish you were toward other drivers while driving to a recent destination. You may find it hard to claim that you were displaying good fruit.

THE MORAL REQUIREMENTS OF THE LAW CAN BE FULFILLED ONLY BY THE SUPERNATURAL WORK OF THE HOLY SPIRIT WITHIN THE NEW COVENANT.

When Paul wrote the above passages to the Galatian church, the Gentiles and Jews of Galatia were struggling with the way they were supposed to go about bearing good fruit. The Jewish believers insisted that the Old Testament law was the key, but the Gentile believers wanted nothing to do with it. Paul stepped in to clarify that it was not an either-or proposition but rather a blend of the two, because the new covenant makes it possible to fulfill the law. The moral requirements of the law can be fulfilled only by the supernatural work of the Holy Spirit within the new covenant.

This settles the question of law versus license, although the same confusion arises to this day. I am thinking of a friend of mine whose husband grew up knowing the things of the Spirit, only to start getting into a "hyper-grace" message—and living according to an attitude that says, "I can do whatever I want because God loves me no matter what." He forgot the part about doing what is pleasing to the Lord. Instead of staying at home and looking after his wife and two children, he spent his evenings at a bar and didn't return home until two in the morning. Before long, some of the deeds of the flesh listed in Galatians appeared in his life, and bad fruit caused havoc in the family.

Clearly, we must strip off the bad fruit and dispose of it without a trace of regret. Repent! (Where have you heard that before?) Then, if the beginnings of bad fruit reappear, we have to turn quickly to the Lord Jesus and ask Him to help nip it in the bud. The apostle Paul's strong urging along these lines is as follows:

> So **put to death the sinful, earthly things lurking within you**. Have nothing to do with sexual immorality, impurity, lust, and evil desires. Don't be greedy, for a greedy person is an idolater, worshiping the things of this world. Because of these sins, the anger of God is coming. You used to do these things when your life was still part of this world. But now is the time to get rid of anger, rage, malicious behavior, slander, and dirty language. Don't lie to each other, for you have stripped off your old sinful nature and all its wicked deeds. **Put on your new nature, and be renewed** as you learn to know your Creator and become like him. In this new life, it doesn't matter if you are a Jew or a Gentile, circumcised or uncircumcised, barbaric, uncivilized, slave, or free. Christ is all that matters, and he lives in all of us.   (Colossians 3:5–11 NLT)

It is not a matter of disposing of bad fruit in order to be acceptable to God, because some amount of bad fruit will continue to make an appearance in your life until the day you die. The key is Christ in you, your hope of glory. (See Colossians 1:27.) He will help you shake the bad fruit off your tree even as He helps you produce better fruit.

WHAT DOES GOOD FRUIT LOOK LIKE?

Paul goes on to prescribe the remedy for bad fruit:

> Since God chose you to be the holy people he loves, you must clothe yourselves with tenderhearted mercy, kindness, humility, gentleness,

and patience. Make allowance for each other's faults, and forgive anyone who offends you. **Remember, the Lord forgave you, so you must forgive others. Above all, clothe yourselves with love,** *which binds us all together in perfect harmony. And let the peace that comes from Christ rule in your hearts. For as members of one body you are called to live in peace. And always be thankful. Let the message about Christ, in all its richness, fill your lives. Teach and counsel each other with all the wisdom he gives. Sing psalms and hymns and spiritual songs to God with thankful hearts.*

(Colossians 3:12–16 NLT)

We want to produce good fruit, in abundance. Besides the characteristics listed in Colossians 3, the Holy Spirit wants to prune and train us until we bear every kind of good fruit we can think of, because, you know…

no good tree bears bad fruit, nor does a bad tree bear good fruit. Each tree is recognized by its own fruit. People do not pick figs from thornbushes, or grapes from briers. A good man brings good things out of the good stored up in his heart, and an evil man brings evil things out of the evil stored up in his heart. For the mouth speaks what the heart is full of. (Luke 6:43–45 NIV)

Consider what is required to grow healthy fruit in the natural. These are no-brainers, but we must consider their parallels in our spiritual lives. You need (1) good soil, (2) plenty of water, (3) adequate sunlight, (4) proper care, and (5) time and patience. The fruit of the Spirit is just as supernatural as the gifts of the Spirit. Although the spiritual gifts are presented as special "grace packages" that are almost like Christmas presents, the same is true of the fruit of the Spirit. Without the grace of God, nobody can bear the good fruit that matures and endures.

Once you are rooted and grounded in the good soil of the Word, and living and growing together with other believers in the body of Christ, it becomes imperative to take stock of the fruit that is being produced in your life. Is it the "fruit of righteousness"? (See Isaiah 32:17 NIV.) Are you ready yet to say that you are finished with bad fruit (i.e., dead to sin)? If so, you are on track! Soon the boughs of your tree will be so heavy with luxuriant, good fruit that you will be compelled to share it with others. The psalmist has painted your portrait: you will be *"like a tree planted by streams of water, which yields its fruit in season and whose leaf does not wither—whatever [you] do prospers"* (Psalm 1:3 NIV).

WITHOUT THE GRACE OF GOD, NOBODY CAN BEAR THE GOOD FRUIT THAT MATURES AND ENDURES.

You will have no worries in years of drought, which *will* come in due time—and surely more than once—because you will never fail to bear the fruit of the life of the Spirit in you. (See Jeremiah 17:7–8.) As you walk with the Lord in newness of life, you will *"live as children of light (for the fruit of the light consists in all goodness, righteousness and truth),"* and you will *"find out what pleases the Lord"* (Ephesians 5:8–10 NIV) so that you can do it. Furthermore, you will *"have nothing to do with the fruitless deeds of darkness, but rather expose them"* (verse 11).

You must endure times of pruning, as with any well-cultivated, fruit-bearing plant, but you will not need to worry about that. Times of pruning indicate that you are worth the Lord's attention and are bearing at least a modest amount of fruit already. He wants to make you able to bear more fruit, if you will agree to the sometimes-painful process of trimming and discarding what seem to be perfectly good boughs and branches. *"Every branch in Me that does not bear fruit, He takes away; and every branch that bears fruit, He prunes it so that it may bear more fruit"* (John 15:2).

The analogy of green, growing things carries through very well. Jesus compared Himself to a healthy vine, and He encouraged each of us to *"abide"* in Him:

> *Abide in Me, and I in you. As the branch cannot bear fruit of itself unless it abides in the vine, so neither can you unless you abide in Me. I am the vine, you are the branches; he who abides in Me and I in him, he bears much fruit, for apart from Me you can do nothing.*
>
> (John 15:4–5)

BEARING THE FRUIT OF THE HOLY SPIRIT

How do we start bearing the fruit of love, joy, peace, patience, kindness, goodness, faithfulness, gentleness, and self-control? Bearing the fruit of the Spirit always begins with a decision of faith in which we say, "Lord, I want to surrender myself to You, from roots to branches."

Let's take a quick look at the nature of the fruit of the Holy Spirit:

Love seeks the highest good for others. Jesus exemplified love, and He taught His disciples how to love. Love is both an action and an emotion; we feel love for God, for ourselves, for other people, and even for things. Remember, God *is* love, everlastingly.

The fruit of *joy* brightens the darkest day. It lifts you up so you can lift up others. Joy is gladness that is not dependent on circumstances but rather depends completely on the Holy Spirit, the Originator of joy. Jesus was *"full of joy through the Holy Spirit"* (Luke 10:21 NIV). While He was on earth, He experienced the emotions of joy and grief alike. (See, for example, John 11:33–35.)

Jesus, known as the Prince of Peace (see Isaiah 9:6), engenders the fruit of *peace* in the hearts of His true disciples. A peaceful heart is free from worry, disturbances, and oppressive thoughts. It is content in all circumstances, according to Philippians 4:11–12. It is not afraid because it is secure and sure of the safekeeping of the Shepherd. (See, for example, Psalm 112:7.)

Patience is a virtuous fruit if ever there was one. Paul praised the *"perfect patience"* of the Lord Jesus, whose long-lasting love outlasted Paul's determination to sin:

> It is a trustworthy statement, deserving full acceptance, that Christ Jesus came into the world to save sinners, among whom I am foremost of all. Yet for this reason I found mercy, so that in me as the foremost, Jesus Christ might demonstrate His perfect patience as an example for those who would believe in Him for eternal life. Now to the King eternal, immortal, invisible, the only God, be honor and glory forever and ever. Amen.   (1 Timothy 1:15–17)

Patience made Jesus slow to avenge the wrongs Paul had committed, waiting and working toward a better outcome. For believers, patience is always available through Christ.

Kindness, the supernatural grace to be merciful, sweet-tempered, and tender, puts others at ease and leads them to the feet of the Father. God expressed His abiding kindness toward us when He sent Jesus Christ to us. (See Ephesians 2:5–7.) Kindness, which has been poured out on us generously through Christ Jesus (see Titus 3:4–7), permeates all the other fruit to make it sweet.

Goodness is the motivation behind selflessness; it makes a person openhearted and generous to others above what they deserve. Scripture exhorts us to *"not grow weary while doing good,"* especially to our brothers and sisters in the body of Christ. (See Galatians 6:9–10 NKJV.) Once you put on Christ, you can be sure that goodness will follow you all the days of your life. (See Psalm 23:6.)

Faithfulness begins with God because He is always and everlastingly faithful. Remember this verse from the book of Revelation? *"I saw heaven opened, and behold, a white horse, and He who sat on it is called Faithful and True"* (Revelation 19:11). He who sits on the heavenly horse is, of course, Jesus Himself. In the Old Testament, we see faithfulness described as a sash around Jesus's waist. (See Isaiah 11:5 NIV.) In us, the fruit of faithfulness is rooted in an unshakable devotion to God; it makes a person dependable, loyal, and full of trust in Him.

The quality or fruit of *gentleness* is not weak or passive or namby-pamby. Jesus is *"gentle and humble in heart."* (See Matthew 11:28–30.) Gentleness is calm. It is nonthreatening. We are invited by the Holy Spirit to let our gentleness be evident to all. (See Philippians 4:5 NIV.) When someone has a gentle spirit, you know that our Lord is near.

The fruit of the Spirit comes from the Holy Spirit and not from anything we can do. That includes the final distinct fruit of the Spirit, *self-control*—it is not something that you and I can achieve solo. However, as with the development of all the fruit, we do need to cooperate with the Spirit as fully as possible.

Only with God's help can we restrain ungodly desires and actions and carry on in harmony with God's will. Self-control is a matter of behavior, both in public and in secret. Where you see angry outbursts, self-control is lacking. (See, for example, Proverbs 29:11.) And unless we are clear-minded and self-controlled, we cannot pray as we ought. (See 1 Peter 4:7.)

I believe that self-control is probably the most overlooked of all of the nine fruit of the Spirit and the most needed in the body of Christ today. We need to cultivate all of these precious fruits in order to walk in the new ways for the new era that is right in front of us.

FEEL THE FRUIT

The fruit of the Spirit is filled with emotions. Yes, you heard me correctly. I did not misspeak. The fruit of the Spirit is filled with emotions! If you think about it in this way, you can see why it is so important to consider the fruit at length when you are learning about how your feelings fit into the big kingdom picture.

Christianity is not only an intellectual or cerebral religion, but also a vibrant, heart-to-heart relationship with the living God. The Feeler realm is very active in the fruit-emotion called love. Just think what a marriage would be like without emotions. Not very lively. Parenting without joy is burdensome. Serving without gladness is boredom. Working without a sense of purpose is monotonous. Sports without the thrill of winning and the sadness of losing would just not be worth it. Music that does not move your heart is just notes on a page.

> ***CHRISTIANITY IS NOT ONLY AN INTELLECTUAL OR CEREBRAL RELIGION, BUT ALSO A VIBRANT, HEART-TO-HEART RELATIONSHIP WITH THE LIVING GOD.***

In short, life would not be worth much without the gift of all kinds of emotions and feelings. We were created in God's image to bear and feel the supernatural fruit of the Spirit—and more. We were made for adventure and excitement and joy, as well as peace and tranquility.

Almost every time the apostle Paul wrote a new epistle to the churches under his care, he opened or closed his letter with blessings and appeals that involve emotions. Just look at this sampling of heartfelt expressions from Paul's letters:

> *I am writing to all of you in Rome who are loved by God and are called to be his own holy people. May God our Father and the Lord Jesus Christ give you grace and peace.* (Romans 1:7 NLT)

> *Greet one another with a holy kiss.* (Romans 16:16)

> *Grace be unto you, and peace, from God our Father, and from the Lord Jesus Christ.* (1 Corinthians 1:3 KJV)

> *Watch, stand fast in the faith, be brave, be strong. Let all that you do be done with love.... I am glad about the coming of Stephanas, Fortunatus, and Achaicus, for what was lacking on your part they supplied. For they refreshed my spirit and yours. Therefore acknowledge such men.... My love be with you all in Christ Jesus.* (1 Corinthians 16:13–14, 17–18, 24 NKJV)

Blessed be the God and Father of our Lord Jesus Christ, the Father of mercies and God of all comfort, who comforts us in all our affliction so that we will be able to comfort those who are in any affliction with the comfort with which we ourselves are comforted by God.

(2 Corinthians 1:3–4)

Finally, brethren, rejoice, be made complete, be comforted, be like-minded, live in peace; and the God of love and peace will be with you. Greet one another with a holy kiss. All the saints greet you. The grace of the Lord Jesus Christ, and the love of God, and the fellowship of the Holy Spirit, be with you all. (2 Corinthians 13:11–14)

I pray that the eyes of your heart may be enlightened in order that you may know the hope to which he has called you, the riches of his glorious inheritance in his holy people. (Ephesians 1:18 NIV)

Peace to the brothers and sisters, and love with faith from God the Father and the Lord Jesus Christ. Grace to all who love our Lord Jesus Christ with an undying love. (Ephesians 6:23–24 NIV)

I thank my God upon every remembrance of you, always in every prayer of mine making request for you all with joy, for your fellowship in the gospel from the first day until now, being confident of this very thing, that He who has begun a good work in you will complete it until the day of Jesus Christ; just as it is right for me to think this of you all, because I have you in my heart, inasmuch as both in my chains and in the defense and confirmation of the gospel, you all are partakers with me of grace. For God is my witness, how greatly I long for you all with the affection of Jesus Christ.

(Philippians 1:3–8 NKJV)

Rejoice in the Lord always. I will say it again: Rejoice! Let your gentleness be evident to all. The Lord is near. Do not be anxious about anything, but in every situation, by prayer and petition, with thanksgiving, present your requests to God. And the peace of God, which transcends all understanding, will guard your hearts and your minds in Christ Jesus. (Philippians 4:4–7 NIV)

We continually ask God to fill you with the knowledge of his will through all the wisdom and understanding that the Spirit gives, so that you may live a life worthy of the Lord and please him in every way: bearing fruit in every good work, growing in the knowledge of God, being strengthened with all power according to his glorious might so that you may have great endurance and patience, and giving joyful thanks to the Father. (Colossians 1:9–12 NIV)

May God himself, the God of peace, sanctify you through and through. May your whole spirit, soul and body be kept blameless at the coming of our Lord Jesus Christ. The one who calls you is faithful, and he will do it. Brothers and sisters, pray for us. Greet all God's people with a holy kiss. I charge you before the Lord to have this letter read to all the brothers and sisters. The grace of our Lord Jesus Christ be with you. (1 Thessalonians 5:23–28 NIV)

To the church of the Thessalonians in God our Father and the Lord Jesus Christ: Grace and peace to you from God the Father and the Lord Jesus Christ. We ought always to thank God for you, brothers and sisters, and rightly so, because your faith is growing more and more, and the love all of you have for one another is increasing. (2 Thessalonians 1:1–3 NIV)

Now may the Lord direct your hearts into the love of God and into the patience of Christ. (2 Thessalonians 3:5 NKJV)

Night and day I constantly remember you in my prayers. Recalling your tears, I long to see you, so that I may be filled with joy. (2 Timothy 1:3–4 NIV)

Paul also wrote, "*For the Kingdom of God is not a matter of what we eat or drink, but of living a life of goodness and peace and joy in the Holy Spirit*" (Romans 14:17 NLT). The kingdom of God is the realm of God's Holy Spirit, and the fruit of the Spirit is supernatural.

Let's abide in Christ Jesus so that His fruit may abound in our lives. As Feelers, Seers, Knowers, and Discerners, we have the joyful privilege of walking in the incredible wonder of bearing the fruit of the Holy Spirit. Let me make this point crystal clear: it is just as supernatural to bear the fruit of the Spirit as it is to move in the gifts of the Spirit. It all originates with the Holy Spirit, and this power is what enables us to be supernaturally natural!

> *IT IS JUST AS SUPERNATURAL TO BEAR THE FRUIT OF THE SPIRIT AS IT IS TO MOVE IN THE GIFTS OF THE SPIRIT.*

IT'S TIME FOR SOME FRUIT!

I love fruit pies, fruit pastries, fruit salad…any dish that's made with fruit is absolutely heavenly to me. I fondly remember my mom asking my dad which kind of fruit pie he liked best. His robust reply was, "I love all fruit pie, especially with a scoop of ice cream on it!"

And, yes, our Father God loves all of the fruit of the Spirit that is cultivated in our lives. Wouldn't it be fun to be able to present to God, as a gift, a huge fruit salad—or even, better yet, a fruit cobbler—of love, joy, peace, patience, kindness, goodness, faithfulness, gentleness, and self-control? Come on, now, you Feelers, let's cook up something really good for God, and let's serve up something really great for the world to come, and *"taste and see that the Lord is good"* (Psalm 34:8).

PRAYER OF A PASSIONATE HEART

Father, in the abundant name of Jesus, help me to grow the supernatural fruit of the Spirit in my life, and increase my ability to use my natural emotions in Your service. I choose to abide in Christ and to let His Word abide in my heart and soul. I choose to die to myself and to live in the realm of the kingdom of God. I awaken my heart and its emotions so that I can more fully experience the love, joy, peace, patience, kindness, goodness, faithfulness, gentleness, and self-control of the Holy Spirit. I declare that I will bear good fruit, fruit that remains, abundant fruit. To the glory of God, and in Jesus's holy name, I pray. Amen.

7

The Gifts of the Spirit

*"Now concerning spiritual gifts, brethren,
I do not want you to be ignorant."*
—1 Corinthians 12:1 (NKJV)

If you are a longtime believer, you may be thinking, "Oh, please, not another rehash of 1 Corinthians 12 and the gifts of the Spirit! I've heard all of this many times before." Why have I included this topic? Actually, in this book focused on the Feeler, we take a fresh look at the gifts of the Spirit—how the gifts look when they "wear" different emotional responses. So, in this chapter, we connect the dots between your spiritual gifts and your emotional makeup.

"Oh, so maybe this won't be the same old, same old. Huh. Intriguing," some of you may now be thinking. You won't be disappointed.

WHAT ARE THE SPIRITUAL GIFTS?

Let's begin with a brief overview, just in case we have some newer believers or those who have been filled with the Holy Spirit more recently. What are the spiritual gifts?

Spiritual gifts are not merely human abilities recast in a spiritual light. They are supernatural "grace packages"—sometimes I call them "gracelets"—sent from our Father God through the Lord Jesus Christ and by the ministry of the Holy Spirit.

In his landmark book *Your Spiritual Gifts Can Help Your Church Grow*, the late C. Peter Wagner, one of my influencers, defined spiritual gifts like this: "A spiritual gift is a special attribute given by the Holy Spirit to every member of the Body of Christ, according to God's grace, for use within the context of the Body."[18]

John Wimber said that the gifts of the Holy Spirit are tools to be used, not toys to be played with. In other words, they are called "gifts" because they are given freely to God's people, but that doesn't mean they are inconsequential.

The gifts of the Spirit are vital to the health of the church. In fact, I firmly believe that it is impossible to have a fully functioning body of Christ apart from the spiritual gifts. Without these supernatural endowments, the church cannot presume to preach the gospel to the whole world, nor can we reap the great harvest prior to the second coming of the Lord. (See, for example, Matthew 9:37–38; Matthew 24:14.) What it comes down to is that these formidable end-time assignments absolutely require the supernatural, divine empowerment of spiritual gifts, operating through as many believers as possible.

IT IS IMPOSSIBLE TO HAVE A FULLY FUNCTIONING BODY OF CHRIST APART FROM THE SPIRITUAL GIFTS.

18. C. Peter Wagner, *Your Spiritual Gifts Can Help Your Church Grow* (Minneapolis, MN: Chosen Books, 2012), 34.

Spiritual gifts are listed in five different places in the New Testament and fall into at least three categories: (1) gifts of the Spirit, (2) ministry gifts, and (3) office gifts:

- 1 Corinthians 12:4–11 (Nine gifts of the Spirit are listed.)
- 1 Corinthians 12:28 (This is a brief comment about the ministry and office gifts of the Spirit.)
- Romans 12:6–8 (This is a partial list of the ministry gifts of the Spirit.)
- 1 Peter 4:10–11 (This is another partial list of the ministry gifts of the Spirit.)
- Ephesians 4:11 (This is a list of the office gifts of the Spirit.)

Below, I have included all five of these passages so you can read them together:

There are different kinds of gifts, but the same Spirit distributes them. There are different kinds of service, but the same Lord. There are different kinds of working, but in all of them and in everyone it is the same God at work. Now to each one the manifestation of the Spirit is given for the common good. To one there is given through the Spirit a message of wisdom, to another a message of knowledge by means of the same Spirit, to another faith by the same Spirit, to another gifts of healing by that one Spirit, to another miraculous powers, to another prophecy, to another distinguishing between spirits, to another speaking in different kinds of tongues, and to still another the interpretation of tongues. All these are the work of one and the same Spirit, and he distributes them to each one, just as he determines. (1 Corinthians 12:4–11 NIV)

God has appointed these in the church: first apostles, second prophets, third teachers, after that miracles, then gifts of healings, helps, administrations, varieties of tongues. (1 Corinthians 12:28 NKJV)

We have different gifts, according to the grace given to each of us. If your gift is prophesying, then prophesy in accordance with your faith; if it is serving, then serve; if it is teaching, then teach; if it is to encourage, then give encouragement; if it is giving, then give generously; if it is to lead, do it diligently; if it is to show mercy, do it cheerfully. (Romans 12:6–8 NIV)

As each one has received a gift, minister it to one another, as good stewards of the manifold grace of God. If anyone speaks, let him speak as the oracles of God. If anyone ministers, let him do it as with the ability which God supplies, that in all things God may be glorified through Jesus Christ. (1 Peter 4:10–11 NKJV)

Now these are the gifts Christ gave to the church: the apostles, the prophets, the evangelists, and the pastors and teachers. (Ephesians 4:11 NLT)

The gifts of the Spirit that we read about in these Scriptures cover much of the specific activity of the Holy Spirit through individuals. In a book such as this one, I cannot go into exhaustive detail about each gift, but you can find many resources that do.[19]

What a wonderful and diverse list of gifts that God gives His people:

+ Wisdom
+ Knowledge
+ Faith
+ Healing
+ Mercy
+ Miraculous powers
+ Prophecy
+ Discernment
+ Generous giving
+ Serving others
+ Administration

19. My book *Releasing Spiritual Gifts Today* (New Kensington, PA: Whitaker House, 2016) provides a thorough discussion of this topic.

- Teaching
- Leadership in the church
- Encouragement
- Tongues
- Interpretation of tongues

In some people, a certain gift really stands out. In most people, blends of gifts develop. But each believer has been given spiritual gifts in some configuration. This includes you, even if you feel your giftedness is limited. These gifts from our living God are alive and growing. Is there anything holding you back from discovering more about your spiritual gifts and stepping out to use them?

These gifts are given by God for the purpose of ministry, specifically for the good of the body of Christ. That is what we learn from 1 Corinthians 12:7, which reads, "*To each one the manifestation of the Spirit is given for the common good*" (NIV). The gifts are the means of building up the body of Christ so that the church will grow and stay healthy. They are intended "*for the equipping of the saints for the work of service, to the building up of the body of Christ*" (Ephesians 4:12).

THE PURPOSE OF THE GIFTS OF THE SPIRIT INCLUDES THE PROCLAMATION AND DEMONSTRATION OF THE GOSPEL OF THE KINGDOM, WHICH IS A SUPERNATURAL ACTIVITY.

The purpose of the gifts of the Spirit also includes the proclamation and demonstration of the gospel of the kingdom, which is a supernatural activity. With the gifts of the Spirit, the members of the body of Christ encourage and equip each other, even as they glorify God. In a corporate setting, congregations can follow the advice of the apostle Paul to the churches: *"What is the outcome then, brethren? When you assemble, each one has a psalm, has a teaching, has a revelation, has a tongue, has an interpretation. Let all things be done for edification"* (1 Corinthians 14:26).

The Source of these gifts is God Himself, who created each one of us to reflect His image in a unique way: *"God always has shown us that these messages are true by signs and wonders and various miracles and by giving certain special abilities from the Holy Spirit to those who believe; yes, God has assigned such gifts to each of us"* (Hebrews 2:4 TLB).

The gifts of the Spirit are also known as the *charismata*, the plural form of the word *charism*, which is from the Greek words *charizesthai* ("to favor or to hand over") and *charis* ("grace"). The reason that the gifts of the Spirit have been distributed so liberally by God is so that no single individual can dominate in the community of the Spirit, otherwise known as the body of Christ or the church. The body needs all of its parts and all of its various gifts:

> *As it is, **there are many parts, but one body**. The eye cannot say to the hand, "I don't need you!" And the head cannot say to the feet, "I don't need you!" On the contrary, those parts of the body that seem to be weaker are indispensable, and the parts that we think are less honorable we treat with special honor. And the parts that are unpresentable are treated with special modesty, while our presentable parts need no special treatment. But God has put the body together, giving greater honor to the parts that lacked it, so that **there should be no division in the body, but that its parts should have equal concern for each other.***
>
> (1 Corinthians 12:20–25 NIV; see also Romans 12:4–8;
> Ephesians 4:1–16; 1 Peter 4:10–11)

MANY GIFTS, MANY ACTIVITIES

We possess and express a wide variety of gifts and present them in a variety of ways depending on our personal makeup, role, geographic location, and the gifts of others used along with ours at any given time.

This is why 1 Corinthians 12 states that not only are there various gifts, but there are also various types of service (ministries) and various ways of manifesting the gifts under the control of the Spirit. (See again 1 Corinthians 12:4–6.)

All of this variety comes from one Source, God Himself—every gift, service, or ministry, and every activity or supernatural manifestation. We have a very generous Father! In fact, looking beyond the Scriptures cited, I have tallied over twenty spiritual gifts altogether, which far exceed the five or the nine gifts that most teachers talk about. The gifts and supporting Scripture references are listed in alphabetical order so they don't appear to be ranked in value or application:

- Administrations (or "steerings")—1 Corinthians 12:28
- Apostle—1 Corinthians 12:28; Ephesians 4:11
- Discerning of spirits—1 Corinthians 12:10
- Eternal life—Romans 6:23 (NKJV, NIV: "...*the gift of God is eternal life in Christ Jesus our Lord.*")
- Evangelist—Ephesians 4:11
- Exhortation or encouragement—Romans 12:8
- Faith—1 Corinthians 12:9
- Giving—Romans 12:8
- Healings, gifts of—1 Corinthians 12:9
- Helps—1 Corinthians 12:28
- Interpretation of tongues—1 Corinthians 12:10; 14:5
- Leadership (or "ruling")—Romans 12:8
- Marriage/celibacy—1 Corinthians 7:7 (TLB: "*I wish everyone could get along without marrying, just as I do. But we are not all the same. God gives some the gift of a husband or wife, and others he gives the gift of being able to stay happily unmarried.*")
- Mercy—Romans 12:8
- Miracles, workings of—1 Corinthians 12:10

+ Pastor (or "shepherd")—Ephesians 4:11

+ Prophecy—1 Corinthians 12:10, 28; 14:1; Ephesians 4:11

+ Righteousness—Romans 5:17 (NKJV: "*...those who receive abundance of grace and of the gift of righteousness will reign in life through the One, Jesus Christ.*")

+ Service—Romans 12:7; 1 Peter 4:11

+ Teaching—Romans 12:7; 1 Corinthians 12:28; Ephesians 4:11

+ Tongues—1 Corinthians 12:10, 28; 1 Corinthians 14

+ Word of knowledge—1 Corinthians 12:8

+ Word of wisdom—1 Corinthians 12:8

As you can see from the references listed after every one of the above Scriptures, each of these gifts of grace is mentioned in the Bible, some of them more than once. And, of course, we see them in action throughout the biblical accounts written about the people of God.

GRACE GIFTS AND CORRESPONDING SENSES

Because this book is about the Feeler realm, I offer my observations about how these spiritual gifts are often expressed in combination with our natural senses.

Discerning of spirits. A good place to start is with the grace gift of discerning of spirits. This is the God-given ability to recognize the identity of the spirits that are behind various manifestations or activities. A person with the gift of discerning of spirits can tell whether a spirit is demonic, human, or divine. Such a person will always need to train their senses to assist in the discernment process. Any of the human senses may come into play, including sight, hearing, touch, taste, smell, and knowing.

Let's say you are stricken with a sudden pain in your forehead. Immediately—because it hurts and because it came "out of nowhere"— you may ask yourself, "What is this headache? Is it just a normal headache? Where did it come from? Why am I feeling it? Is it from the evil one, maybe a territorial spirit of some sort? Or is it because I am feeling stressed out these days? Or could it be an indication that someone in this room needs to be healed of a headache, and the Spirit wants me to pray for that person?"

Then you drill down farther: "The pain is right behind my eyes, but I can't think of any recent eyestrain, nor have I been squinting in bright lights. And I don't usually get headaches like this. However [with a sudden "knowing"], I think this relates to my gift of prophecy. The evil one is coming against the eyes of this seer, trying to dissuade and discourage me from using that gift. That's it!"

Having discerned the source of the headache, you can then decide, with the help of the Holy Spirit, how to resist the devil so that he will flee from you. (See James 4:7.)

THE DISCERNING OF SPIRITS IS THE GOD-GIVEN ABILITY TO RECOGNIZE THE IDENTITY OF THE SPIRITS THAT ARE BEHIND VARIOUS MANIFESTATIONS OR ACTIVITIES.

Word of knowledge. Through the gift of a word of knowledge, God shares with one of His children a small portion of His complete knowledge. It is not possible to ascertain this revelatory information about a person or a situation by the exercise of the natural mind; the revelation is a gift. However, sorting out the information does require a well-trained mind and perceptive senses.

Some people receive words of knowledge by their sense of *knowing*; they "just know" a thing. But some people will "see" a word or words in their mind's eye. Others will "feel" their way to the revelation, noticing physical sensations, especially when the revelation relates to the operation of gifts of healings or workings of miracles. When a person is not simply receiving a supernatural download of information, the gift usually operates within the Feeler realm, empathetically, as pains or other sensations are manifested in their body.

One good test of the accuracy of such a revelation is this: if you speak out the word of knowledge, and the pain or sensation ceases, then you can be sure that it came from the Holy Spirit. One moment, you are feeling something significant, and that sensation ceases as soon as you acknowledge a word of knowledge and release it. This has been my experience.

Word of wisdom. The gift of a word of wisdom is the God-given ability to articulate life-changing insights into God's mysterious purposes for humankind, both on a global scale and on an individual level. Knowledge provides the facts, but wisdom shows you what to do with those facts.

Here again, a Feeler's sense of knowing is a primary avenue for the exercise of the gift. They "just know" the wisdom application for the situation. Other times, the Feeler will see, hear, or taste something in a vision or a dream, and understand how to interpret it as a word of wisdom. I can sometimes feel the "spirit of wisdom" come onto me, and I can also feel it lift. Often, I feel a sensation around my head as though I am being crowned with understanding. Other times, it appears to be more like a mantle of authority that comes and sits on my shoulders, and I realize I have been granted supernatural wisdom to resolve a difficult problem.

A person who exercises the gift of a word of wisdom can identify with the following prophecy of Isaiah about the Messiah:

> *The Spirit of the* LORD *will rest on Him, the spirit of wisdom and understanding, the spirit of counsel and strength, the spirit of knowledge and the fear of the* LORD. *And He will delight in the fear of the* LORD, *and He will not judge by what His eyes see, nor make a decision by what His ears hear; but with righteousness He will judge....* (Isaiah 11:2–4)

It is absolutely vital to the ongoing spread of God's kingdom on earth to be able to bring heavenly wisdom to bear on earthly concerns.

Faith. I know what it feels like to have supernatural faith come upon me and into me. This is different from the "saving" kind of faith or our daily "walking in grace" faith. The gift of faith is bestowed for special purposes, even miracles. It is an amazing dimension.

This kind of faith often comes with a surge of assurance, and it combines the senses of knowing and feeling. When you receive a surge of confidence that God not only can but will perform a particular action, it's as if a feeling of sureness is flowing into you like a river of living water. This is not the same as self-confidence. It is a God-confidence that rises up within you, and you know that you know that you know. You just know that things are going to change for the better!

You sit or stand up straighter, and you activate your faith by releasing the flow—expressing it verbally in some way. Remember, it is out of the heart that the mouth speaks. (See, for example, Luke 6:45.) Faith *speaks*. Be alert and watch for any surge of faith that rises up out of your innermost being so that you can release a decree that things will change.

Gifts of healings. Scripture refers to the "gifts of healings"—both words are plural in the Greek—because of the multiplicity of types of healings that God can bring. Very often, gifts of healings seem to be revealed through a person's physical senses. You may feel a sensation of heat or a physical vibration or a surge of power. You may well find divine compassion rising up in your heart. You may see a sheen on someone's skin or a light shining on a part of the person's body. You may hear a key word or phrase or "just know" what God wants to heal. You may catch a scent of flowers where there is no natural explanation for it. Any of your senses can come into play.

With me, my natural senses become heightened or illuminated, and so can yours. I feel the pain; I know the source; in a vision, I see the organ that needs to be healed; I hear a specific word; I can smell the demonic source of the foul spirit. It is possible for anyone to learn to do this—such heightened senses are not limited to only highly gifted persons.

The healing itself may come as soon as you pray for it, or even before you pray. Or it may manifest itself over a period of time. Either way, the gift will have released the healing touch of Jesus, and the one who is healed will feel it.

Workings of miracles. The gift of the working of miracles is the God-given ability to cooperate with God as He performs miracles. He is the Instigator and the Fulfiller of the action, while you, as a human being, will participate in whatever manner is appropriate. Of necessity, your senses will come into play as you observe the miracle from beginning to end. Sometimes, your senses will be enhanced supernaturally. Your palms might exude anointing oil or you might catch a glimpse of something with X-ray vision.

Almost certainly, you will be inundated with a sense of sureness or confidence in God's sovereign power as you see it being applied to an "impossible" situation. Some people have an almost Clark-Kent-to-Superman experience as a sense of boldness comes upon them and they step out to activate a breakthrough. Please note: you will have to step out of your comfort zone in order to work the miracle.

Always remember that the gifts of the Spirit are often coupled together. They are like the colors of the rainbow—there is no clear demarcation showing where one ends and the next one begins. So, we find miracles on one side of faith and gifts of healings on the other side of faith.

Tongues and interpretation of tongues. The gift of tongues is a vocal miracle that enables people to speak and pray in a language they have never learned. Most of the time, the language seems to be a heavenly one that is unidentifiable, at least in its present context; however, occasionally, people who speak out in tongues find that they have declared the good news to native speakers who understand the language being spoken.

When this gift operates in conjunction with the gift of interpretation of tongues, divine revelation enables the speaker—or, more often, another person—to speak, in the local language, the message that was just uttered in tongues. In a corporate setting, the gift of interpretation usually manifests when a message in tongues is spoken. This is not often a word-for-word translation but rather an expression of the overall gist of the message.

> **THE GIFTS OF THE SPIRIT ARE LIKE THE COLORS OF THE RAINBOW—THERE IS NO CLEAR DEMARCATION SHOWING WHERE ONE ENDS AND THE NEXT ONE BEGINS.**

The gift of tongues is completely transrational—beyond rational. To the recipient, it can become unimpressive and routine over time, yet when it is first received in conjunction with being filled with the Spirit, many euphoric sensations can be felt. Some people report feeling an electric tingling. Others will see words imprinted in the air and will "read" them, or hear in their heads specific, unfamiliar words that they are able to repeat. As they move out in faith, they achieve fluency in speaking with the gift of tongues.

In a similar way, people who are interpreting a message in tongues may "just know" what to say, or they may see or hear key words, often with a sense of heightened acuity in the presence of God's glory. When this gift is operating, your spirit will bear witness to God's presence. Calming peace coupled with quiet joy will move in so that you can feel it.

The key is to keep going with the flow. To move from speaking in tongues into the interpretation of tongues, don't stop to rationalize. I have found that if I stop, the flow of the revelatory river stops. I may well feel the desire to move on from an utterance in tongues right into the interpretation, but if I stop speaking, the shift from the supernatural language to English (in my case) does not occur.

Prophecy. The gift of prophecy includes a supernaturally imparted ability to hear from the Holy Spirit and to speak God's counsel not only to an assembled group of believers, but also to individuals. Its three main purposes are as follows: (1) to edify or to build up hearers, (2) to exhort or encourage hearers, and (3) to comfort or cheer up those who receive the prophetic word.

As with all of the vocal gifts of the Spirit, a number of human senses can come into play alongside a prophetic sense. A prophet may feel waves of God's presence, a sense of urgency, a hunch, or even a "rising up" sensation. They may see a vision, notice an unusual smell, or even hear audible words being spoken.

I have written more on this gift and subject than any of the rest because prophecy is my primary calling and gifting. (For more, see my books *The Prophet*, *The Seer*, and *The Discerner*.[20] With the addition of *The Feeler*, I hope to touch, if not cover, all four bases in the game so that you can learn to hit the ball out of the park!)

TUNING IN

In my own experience, *feeling* has been an operative word from the very beginning. Back in the days of the Jesus People Movement, I participated in prayer gatherings. While the group worshiped with guitars and tambourines, I sat on the floor with my eyes shut. Or I sat with my eyes open but not looking at anybody in particular, just sort of tuning in to God. I didn't realize that people were looking at me, or I might have shut it down. I was just trying to respond to the feelings I was getting.

I would feel the presence of God in my hands. I would sit in the meeting and start rubbing my hands together. I was getting in touch with the river of God within me and tuning in to the tangible presence

---

20. *The Prophet* (Shippensburg, PA: Destiny Image, 2019; *The Seer*, expanded edition (Shippensburg, PA: Destiny Image, 2012); *The Discerner* (New Kensington, PA: Whitaker House, 2017).

of God around me and coming upon me. When there was a pause in the worship, which tended to happen when other people looked in my direction and noticed my demeanor, I often had a word from God. Even as a reluctant and unwitting twenty-year-old prophet, I felt the anointing rise, and I released an inspirational word appropriate for the moment. After I shared the word, I felt the grace lift.

That was my experience. Everyone's experience is different. Each of us has an inclination to "tune in" in a particular way, and if we find ourselves in an environment where we can express or release a word—if only in the form of a simple, inspired prayer—we can begin to practice using our gifts, sometimes even before we know what those gifts are called.

ASK GOD FOR WISDOM ON HOW TO EXPRESS YOUR SPIRITUAL GIFTS IN A GIVEN SETTING, AND HE WILL GRANT IT.

We are not tuning in to a radio frequency; we are tuning in *relationally* to the Lord Himself. And while we can learn from each other how to do it, and while we must respect the culture in which we find ourselves, we should always be careful not to let our expression of a spiritual gift be completely prescribed by the culture of the group. Follow the cultural rules as much as possible, but always be aware that God's possibilities are unlimited. For example, if a group insists on using only the King James Version of the Bible, okay. If their definition of "*decently and in order*" (1 Corinthians 14:40 NKJV, KJV) differs from yours, just respect it and work within it. If they don't allow speaking out loud in tongues without an interpretation, and you feel led to speak out, ask a person in charge what to do.

Just don't let such rules limit the way you reach up to God. Ask Him for wisdom on how to express your spiritual gifts in a given setting, and He will grant it. As the Word reminds us, *"If any of you lacks wisdom, let him ask of God, who gives to all liberally and without reproach, and it will be given to him"* (James 1:5 NKJV). As you grow in your confidence in exercising a particular spiritual gift, you may feel led to break out of the box. Listen to the Lord and "feel it out."

The exercise of many spiritual gifts is a hidden thing, anyway—I'm thinking of such gifts as service or giving—so you won't have to worry as much about how others will receive your input.

Always be open to correction and adjustments along the way. Do everything with love. *"Let love be your greatest aim; nevertheless, ask also for the special abilities the Holy Spirit gives, and especially the gift of prophecy, being able to preach the messages of God"* (1 Corinthians 14:1 TLB). Above all, never, ever stop seeking the Giver!

ACCOMPANYING SENSATIONS

As I have been explaining in this chapter, the gifts of the Spirit are received and released by faith, often with accompanying sensations that can be felt.[21]

Seer-prophet Bob Jones, who has now graduated to his eternal, heavenly reward, was more at home in heaven than most people when he was still on earth. He was one of my mentors in understanding how to sense the Lord at work. Many times, we would hear him say things like the following:

"Did you feel the wind on that? That's the Spirit bearing witness."

"Oh, the fire is on that word!"

"Feel the heat. That is the healing presence of Jesus."

"I have to wait until I feel the unction to function."

---

21. For more teaching in these areas, see my related books *Releasing Spiritual Gifts Today*; *Living a Supernatural Life* (Minneapolis, MN: Chosen Books, 2013); and *Hearing God's Voice Today* (Minneapolis, MN: Chosen Books, 2016).

"There it comes. His power is going into you right now. Did you feel that?"

"Someone's ears just popped open. Who is hearing from God right now?"

"Faith is here now. I can feel it rising up from my belly."

I have found that the feeling of wind in a room can indicate the activity of angels, in accordance with Hebrews 1:7, 14. The sensing of "fire" on a word or on a person can show the empowerment of the Holy Spirit. Heat (usually in your hands) can be a sign that the healing power of Jesus is ready to flow freely.

As already mentioned, a feeling of pain in a part of your body may point to an imminent healing for another person that relates to that part of the body. A feeling of weight coming down on your shoulders may signify that the government of God is manifesting; it may be God's way of saying to you, "You are now walking in spiritual leadership. It is from Me, so don't back away from it." Similarly, a feeling of a burden may reveal an assignment to carry a person or a purpose in intercessory prayer.

All of your senses can be used by God in conjunction with spiritual gifts. For example, if you hear an alarm going off, it may be a way of knowing that it's time to alert the people of God to some threat. A feeling of pain behind the eye (yours or someone else's) may mean that witchcraft is involved in a situation. A feeling of muffled hearing may signify that a deaf and dumb spirit is lurking behind a person's problem.

I'm sure that if I asked a group of seasoned, Spirit-filled ministers for other examples, they could come up with many more. The main ideas are simply that your physical senses are your gateways into the spiritual realm and that you should invite the Holy Spirit to tutor you in making the appropriate connections.

Last but not least, I want to mention the feeling that accompanies any use of a spiritual gift. Our Father God delights to give us gifts:

If you then, being evil, know how to give good gifts to your children, how much more will your Father who is in heaven give what is good to those who ask Him!   (Matthew 7:11)

Every good thing given and every perfect gift is from above, coming down from the Father of lights.   (James 1:17)

No doubt, you know how good it feels to give someone a gift. *"Remember the words of the Lord Jesus, that He said, 'It is more blessed to give than to receive'"* (Acts 20:35 NKJV). Givers feel a sense of pleasure and happiness, sometimes even more joy than the recipients of their gifts. With the giving of gifts, feelings rise up, feelings such as joy, peace, satisfaction, compassion, benediction, and delight.

It is no different with spiritual gifts. God feels good about giving them to us, and we feel good when we use them. Let's rejoice that we can share such a wealth of goodness!

PRAYER OF A PASSIONATE HEART

Father, in the gracious name of Jesus, I choose to make love my aim and to earnestly desire the spiritual gifts. Holy Spirit, baptize me with Your presence and power. Fill me to overflowing with Your anointing. I choose to let the river of God flow into me and out of me to the world around me. Enlighten and illuminate my senses so I can know the moving of Your Spirit in these realms. More than before, I want to move in the vocal, revelatory, and power gifts of Your Holy Spirit. Teach me the ways of a Feeler so that I can move more effectively under the direction of Your Holy Spirit. Thank You, and amen.

8

The Power of Conviction

"And He, when He comes, will convict the world concerning
sin and righteousness and judgment."
—John 16:8

Conviction. The missing ingredient in today's modern church culture is the experiential convicting work of the Holy Spirit concerning sin, righteousness, and the judgment to come. Without this necessary, piercing ministry of the Holy Spirit, we might be left to another round of renewal gatherings only.

Now that I've made that stark statement, let's look at the role our emotions play in the experience of being humbled before God's holiness. I realize that people seldom choose to dwell on the feelings that overtake us when we are convicted of our sin because it makes us feel uncomfortable, too often reminding us of our wretched humanness and our desperate separation from God. Yet emotions—those of heartbreak and delight alike—are keys of true conviction, and of the true personal revival that accompanies it.

Those uncomfortable feelings drive us into the Lord's saving arms. And once we come close to Him, our tears of sorrow turn into tears of gratitude and joy.

CONVICTION

What does conviction mean in the context of the Christian life?

Conviction is not much different from what it means in the legal sense, where, in a court of law, a conviction is a formal declaration of guilt for a criminal act. There, a conviction is handed down by a jury or a judge, as in, "He was convicted of first-degree murder," or "She had a previous conviction for a similar offense."

It's also similar to another way the word *conviction* is employed in common usage—to describe a firmly held belief or opinion. Three examples: "She takes great pride in stating her political convictions"; "It is his conviction that his daughter's death was no accident"; "The tone of his voice lacked conviction."

We find the word used in both the Old and the New Testament, sometimes in an ordinary way with reference to a declaration of blame or a firmly held opinion, and sometimes as the best way of describing what happens when the Holy Spirit declares to us the guilt of our sinfulness and convinces us of it, beyond our ability to shake it off.

The following is a sampling of passages that use the word to describe ordinary human convictions:

*One witness is not enough to **convict** anyone accused of any crime or offense they may have committed. A matter must be established by the testimony of two or three witnesses.* (Deuteronomy 19:15 NIV)

*I was forty years old when Moses the servant of the LORD sent me from Kadesh Barnea to explore the land. And I brought him back a report according to my **convictions**.* (Joshua 14:7 NIV)

*One of the prisoners at that time was Barabbas, **convicted** along with others for murder during an insurrection.* (Mark 15:7 TLB)

*Then Nicodemus spoke up.... "Is it legal to **convict** a man before he is even tried?" he asked.* (John 7:50–51 TLB)

*Which of you **convicts** Me of sin? And if I tell the truth, why do you not believe Me?* (John 8:46 NKJV)

*I quickly pointed out to them that Roman law does not **convict** a man before he is tried. He is given an opportunity to defend himself face-to-face with his accusers.* (Acts 25:16 TLB)

*The faith which you have, have as your own **conviction** before God. Happy is he who does not condemn himself in what he approves.* (Romans 14:22)

*Now faith is the assurance of things hoped for, the **conviction** of things not seen.* (Hebrews 11:1)

Then, too, there are biblical verses in which variations of the word *convict* are used in connection with the work of the Holy Spirit:

*Nevertheless I tell you the truth. It is to your advantage that I go away; for if I do not go away, the Helper will not come to you; but if I depart, I will send Him to you. And when He has come, He will **convict** the world of sin, and of righteousness, and of judgment.* (John 16:7–8 NKJV)

*But if all prophesy, and an unbeliever or an uninformed person comes in, he is convinced by all, he is **convicted** by all.* (1 Corinthians 14:24 NKJV)

*Our gospel did not come to you in word only, but also in power and in the Holy Spirit and with full **conviction**.* (1 Thessalonians 1:5)

What we learn from these scriptural usages is that *conviction* is a strong word, whether it is being used in a human or a divine sense. Conviction *does* something. At the least, it means that your personal opinion has been firmed up and fortified, or that your guilt over an identifiable misdemeanor has been confirmed by others. At the most, conviction means that the God of the universe, whose "court of law" declares each and every one of us profoundly guilty of a sinful state of being that He finds offensive, has once again swooped into a human soul to both convict—and rescue.

Which brings us to the idea of revival.

REVIVAL RESULTS FROM CONVICTION

A vital aspect of the Holy Spirit's ministry is to bring the conviction of sin to individual men and women. This is in addition to His ministry of distributing the gifts of the Spirit and bringing to fruition the fruit of the Spirit in human lives. Many believers have written and preached and taught about the multifaceted ministry of the Holy Spirit, but I believe that His ministry of bringing the conviction of sin has often been neglected.

Watch out when the Spirit comes into your world with conviction *"concerning sin and righteousness and judgment"* (John 16:8)![22] His conviction is irresistible, both in a positive and in a negative sense. He will put His mighty thumb down hard on your self-important sin, and He will cause you to see it as you have never seen it before—as utterly offensive in the light of the perfection of your Creator. He will also supply you with supernatural grace so that you can respond properly, even to a crushing revelation. For your sake, and far beyond what you deserve, He brings the overwhelming love of God to bear against your sin, forgiving you and pulling you up out of it.

He doesn't come to destroy you; He comes to save you. Your sin is what would sooner or later destroy you, because nothing about it can ever put your feet on the path of salvation and true joy. The Holy Spirit comes at just the right time and in just the right way to convince and convict you of this truth. He supplies you with all of the raw material for saving faith, and then He molds it together for you.

---

22. You can explore the idea of the judgment of God in my book *Radical Faith: Essentials for Spirit-Filled Believers* (Minneapolis, MN: Chosen Books, 2011).

He does this not only when you first bow to the lordship of Christ in your life, but all along the way, as needed. Sin has killed off something within you, and He revives you. You were dead in your sin, and He raises you from the dead. When He comes like this, your emotions become inflamed with a combination of remorse and alarm and repentance—along with incredible relief and eager submission. Nobody can come through the fire of the Holy Spirit's conviction passively or with clinical objectivity. It is an emotional experience. You are so sad, and then you are so glad. You are laid low, and then you are raised up high.

MANY BELIEVERS HAVE WRITTEN AND PREACHED AND TAUGHT ABOUT THE MULTIFACETED MINISTRY OF THE HOLY SPIRIT, BUT I BELIEVE THAT HIS MINISTRY OF BRINGING THE CONVICTION OF SIN HAS OFTEN BEEN NEGLECTED.

Revival! Revival means the recovery of life to something that was dead or seemingly dead, such as the revival of a drowned person. If you think about it, you realize that "revival" can never apply to situations where there was never any life in the first place, because it means coming *back* to life. Dead bodies were once alive, and they can be revived by God. Long-gone dreams can be restored and revitalized. Long-neglected truth and obedience can come back into circulation. Apathy and inattention can be reanimated. Faith and commitment that have been on life support can be reinstated and energized.

In the historic church, revival means that new life surges into the body of Christ. Faith is renewed, and joy springs up. With the prompting of the Holy Spirit, people begin to work together again as a body. Everything seems fresh and exciting. Emotions run high.[23]

You can't expect to have a revival without emotion. Emotions animate people. Thus, when God sends revival to reanimate the church, people will express their joy—or their alarm, if they don't happen to like what they see. Either way, when revival hits, no longer can they remain the "frozen chosen"!

CONVICTION: KEY TO REVIVAL

The people of God invite Him to come and bring revival, regardless of what that may look like. Revival of life can become messy, just as life itself is messy. With the psalmist, people *ask* the Holy Spirit to come and clean house. "Revive us again!" they cry out:

> *Restore us, O God of our salvation, and cause Your anger toward us to cease. Will You be angry with us forever? Will You prolong Your anger to all generations? Will You not revive us again, that Your people may rejoice in You?* (Psalm 85:4–6 NKJV)

They are praying, "Pull out the stops, Lord! Shake us and purify us and terrify us and carry us with You into battle! Have mercy on Your people. We need You desperately!"

> *Oh, that You would rend the heavens! That You would come down! That the mountains might shake at Your presence—as fire burns brushwood, as fire causes water to boil—to make Your name known to Your adversaries, that the nations may tremble at Your presence! When You did awesome things for which we did not look, You came down, the mountains shook at Your presence. For since the beginning of the world men have not heard nor perceived by the ear, nor has the eye seen any God besides You, who acts for the one who waits for Him.* (Isaiah 64:1–4 NKJV)

---

23. In church history, you can find five outstanding characteristics of classic revivals: (1) a passionate denunciation of sin, (2) a revelation of God's holiness, (3) a deep awareness of the love and mercy of God, (4) a heightened consciousness of eternity, and (5) an experiential conviction of sin.

LORD, I have heard of your fame; I stand in awe of your deeds, LORD. Repeat them in our day, in our time make them known; in wrath remember mercy. (Habakkuk 3:2 NIV)

Such prayers have always worked. In both the Old and the New Testaments, testimony of God's faithfulness follows closely after the plea for revival:

If my people, who are called by my name, will humble themselves and pray and seek my face and turn from their wicked ways, then I will hear from heaven, and I will forgive their sin and will heal their land. (2 Chronicles 7:14 NIV)

Repent, then, and turn to God, so that your sins may be wiped out, that times of refreshing may come from the Lord, and that he may send the Messiah, who has been appointed for you—even Jesus. (Acts 3:19–20 NIV)

These verses, along with many others, have been prayed throughout generations as the "forerunners" intercede for revival. Their prayers go ahead of revival, breaking open a territory for God. Conviction falls on people as they become aware of their sinful, hopeless condition and their urgent need to "get right with God."[24] How can the vast chasm be bridged between an all-righteous God and corrupted, selfish men and women? Only by the conviction and subsequent action of the Holy Spirit, who brings the kingdom of God to earth and, with it, renewed life.

On what important transaction does revival depend? Repentance, which follows the conviction of sin. God's people, whether individually or corporately, cannot be revived unless they abandon their death-dealing attachments to sin. Once the Holy Spirit brings conviction, and they respond wholeheartedly, then revival can be planted and new growth can flourish.

---

24. Conviction is not the same as condemnation. When a feeling of condemnation is stirred up by the evil one, it leads you down, not up. It is a hopeless dead end rather than a bridge to God's life.

GOD'S PEOPLE, WHETHER INDIVIDUALLY OR CORPORATELY, CANNOT BE REVIVED UNLESS THEY ABANDON THEIR DEATH-DEALING ATTACHMENTS TO SIN.

Conviction can come upon a person quietly, in a way that outsiders would not notice, even as the convicted person is undergoing a silent revolution inside. Often, however, we see people responding in an emotional, almost convulsive, way, as recorded in documents such as David Brainerd's journal of his work with the native inhabitants of colonial New Jersey:

Aug. 6. In the morning I discoursed to the Indians at the house where I lodged: many of them were then much affected, and appeared surprisingly tender, so that a few words about their souls' concerns would cause the tears to flow freely, and produce many sobs and groans.

In the afternoon, they being returned to the place where I had usually preached amongst them, I again discoursed to them there. There were about fifty-five persons in all, about forty that were capable of attending divine service with understanding. I insisted upon 1 John iv. 10. "Herein is love," &c. They seemed eager of hearing; but there appeared nothing very remarkable, except their attention, till near the close of my discourse; and then divine truths were attended with a surprising influence, and produced a great concern among them. There was scarce three in forty that could refrain from tears and bitter cries. They all, as one, seemed in an agony of soul to obtain an interest in Christ; and the more I discoursed of the love and compassion of God in sending his Son to suffer for the sins of men, and the more I invited them to come and partake of his love, the more their distress was aggravated, because they felt themselves unable to come. — It was surprising to see how their hearts seemed to be pierced with the tender and melting invitations of the gospel, when there was not a word of terror spoken to them.[25]

In our day, we have seen this kind of response to conviction in churches such as the Brownsville Assembly of God in Pensacola, Florida, which experienced a dramatic revival under the scorching preaching of Evangelist Steve Hill and Pastor John Kilpatrick in the mid- to late 1990s:

> Concerning the revival, [Brownsville Assembly pastor] John Kilpatrick reported:
>
>> Corporate businessmen in expensive suits kneel and weep uncontrollably as they repent of secret sins. Drug addicts and prostitutes fall to the floor on their faces beside them, to lie prostrate before God as they confess Jesus as Lord for the first time in their lives. Reserved elderly women and weary young mothers dance unashamedly before the Lord with joy. They have been forgiven. Young children see incredible visions of Jesus, their faces a picture of divine delight framed by slender arms raised heavenward.[26]

Revival comes in response to hunger for God and for holiness. Hunger is a strong feeling. Fervent prayers before, during, and after a time of revival express the anointed emotional response of seekers. Most of them are not getting swept up in group hysteria, because the Holy Spirit has established a connection with each one of them. He is dealing with them on an individual basis. Each person's sins and failings are unique and distinct, and God reaches out via His Spirit to address their particular irregularities. Isn't that remarkable?

25. *David Brainerd's Journal, Part I, from AD 1745 June 19 to Nov 4, at Crossweeksung and Forks of Delaware*, The NTSLibrary, http://www.ntslibrary.com/brainerd_journal.pdf.
26. As quoted in "1995 – Brownsville Revival," on the website Beautiful Feet, https://romans1015.com/brownsville-revival (accessed September 14, 2020).

More than that, it is absolutely revolutionary. When big stuff is happening in people's hearts, no wonder there are tears—both anguished and ecstatic—and emotional outbursts. Even the "peace that surpasses understanding" (see Philippians 4:7), which envelops some people after conviction and repentance, is an emotional response—pure satisfaction and calm joy.

EXPRESSIVE AND EMOTIONAL

There is no getting away from the fact that conviction of sin, repentance, and subsequent renewal and revival are expressive and emotional. Even relatively sober and stern individuals find that their hearts are "strangely warmed," to borrow a phrase from John Wesley. Inevitably, passions are stirred in the hearts of all involved in a move of the Holy Spirit.

Often, it starts with a passionate denunciation of sin by a preacher. He or she does not mince words, recognizing that Jesus Himself denounced sin in no mild terms. After all, we know that He said to the Pharisees, *"You brood of vipers, how can you who are evil say anything good?"* (Matthew 12:34 NIV). And remember how He drove the money-changers out of the temple? Talk about emotion—anger, indignation, outrage, fury:

> When He had made a whip of cords, He drove them all out of the temple, with the sheep and the oxen, and poured out the changers' money and overturned the tables. And He said to those who sold doves, "Take these things away! Do not make My Father's house a house of merchandise!"   (John 2:15–16 NKJV)

Jesus's half brother James seemed to lash out at people who were sitting on the fence of commitment to God, insulting them by comparing them to adulterers: *"Adulterers and adulteresses! Do you not know that friendship with the world is enmity with God? Whoever therefore wants to be a friend of the world makes himself an enemy of God"* (James 4:4 NKJV). So, we see that feelings of anger are not always wrong and that there really is such a thing as righteous anger!

Throughout Christian history, preachers have roared like lions against sin. I'm thinking of George Whitefield, whose booming voice and convicting words penetrated the hearts of listeners in eighteenth-century England and America, whether the listeners intended to heed him consciously or not. The Holy Spirit used Whitefield like a megaphone. Sin is an enemy, and it must be denounced as such.

Such a passionate denunciation of sin comes from an equally passionate awareness of the unapproachable holiness of God. Jonathan Edwards, like George Whitefield and David Brainerd, was caught up in the First Great Awakening and preached sermon after sermon about holiness. His description of the contrast between heaven and hell aroused strong reactions in people.

According to eyewitness reports, Edwards was unemotional to a fault in his demeanor, but that did not blunt the effect of his words on his hearers. To this day, he is better known for the convicting sermon "Sinners in the Hands of an Angry God" than for anything else.[27] He himself simply read off the text on the page in front of him, while the listeners reacted with terror, as if hell itself had opened up beneath their feet. The conviction of the Holy Spirit provoked a remarkable emotional and spiritual response within them. It was as though this scene, described in Revelation 20, was playing on a big screen in the church:

> *I saw a great white throne, and him that sat on it, from whose face the earth and the heaven fled away; and there was found no place for them…. And they were judged every man according to their works…. And whosoever was not found written in the book of life was cast into the lake of fire.* (Revelation 20:11, 13, 15 KJV)

To the congregation, this was very real and very immediate. And guess what? Their violent emotions drove them to Jesus. Not only were they afraid of suffering the torments of hell, but they were also convicted of their utter need of a Savior, whose mercy and love drew them

---

27. Other Jonathan Edwards sermon titles include "Wrath Upon the Wicked for the Uttermost" and "Eternity of Hell's Torments." Besides showing a passionate awareness of the unapproachable holiness of God, many of his sermons reveal a heightened consciousness of eternity.

irresistibly. They may have trembled with fear at first, but then they would have trembled with awe in the presence of the One who had come to rescue them from certain destruction. Without their emotional reactions, very little of lasting significance would have occurred.

Still trembling, they would have echoed these words of Paul:

Who shall separate us from the love of Christ? Shall trouble or hardship or persecution or famine or nakedness or danger or sword? As it is written: "For your sake we face death all day long; we are considered as sheep to be slaughtered." No, in all these things we are more than conquerors through him who loved us. For I am convinced that neither death nor life, neither angels nor demons, neither the present nor the future, nor any powers, neither height nor depth, nor anything else in all creation, will be able to separate us from the love of God that is in Christ Jesus our Lord.   (Romans 8:35–39 NIV)

EXPERIENTIAL CONVICTION OF SIN

This kind of dramatic conviction and conversion experience is the work of the Holy Spirit, and so it is a gentler experience. In every case, an encounter with the Holy Spirit arouses an emotional response. And such encounters are not reserved for an elite few, such as the Old Testament patriarchs; they are for everyone.

Jesus guaranteed that all generations would have access to God through the gift of His Holy Spirit. Remember what He told His disciples before His crucifixion:

I tell you the truth. It is to your advantage that I go away; for if I do not go away, the Helper will not come to you; but if I depart, I will send Him to you. And when He has come, He will convict the world of sin, and of righteousness, and of judgment. (John 16:7–8 NKJV)

Again, I'm not referring to only an experiential conviction of sin in a person's initial conversion, but also the conviction of sin and God's holiness that is meant to be part of our ongoing experience with God.

As I hope you know firsthand, we don't emerge from a conversion experience or from the baptismal waters in a perfectly sanctified state. Far from it. To keep close to God, believers require the frequent nudging and prodding of the Shepherd's staff. We can *feel* it. With our emotions, we respond to it, possibly with resistant stubbornness but more likely with humble submission, when our hearts just fall down before Him. Whether we are listening to a sermon in a congregational setting or alone at home reading the Bible, a word of truth penetrates our awareness like a shaft of light—and we can't ignore it.

The Holy Spirit softens our hearts and penetrates our souls. Emotionally, we *feel* the weight of conviction. We have the gut feeling that a particular thing is deeply displeasing to God and that we must rectify it. Convinced that we must confess our sin, we repent of it and ask His help to change our attitudes, actions, and lifestyles.

We may feel weepy. We may even enter into a time of anguished soul-travail. We may long to escape the fears and misery that threaten to overpower us.

> **EMOTIONALLY, WE FEEL THE WEIGHT OF CONVICTION. WE HAVE THE GUT FEELING THAT A PARTICULAR THING IS DEEPLY DISPLEASING TO GOD AND THAT WE MUST RECTIFY IT.**

The Holy Spirit never overwhelms us with too much at once. Rather, one step at a time, He keeps us on God's straight and narrow path. His course corrections become part of our testimony, and we learn to value them highly. Our interactions with Him—even when He must convict us of sin quite often—become precious to us. In a remarkable way, the emotional pain of an experience of Holy Spirit-inspired conviction tastes almost sweet. He cares about me! This is a demonstration of true love. He is protecting me from my own sinful desires and bad decisions! He is saving me once again. Thank You, Father; thank You, Jesus; and thank You, Holy Spirit!

We rejoice in the truth. Forgiveness is guaranteed. No longer will God hold our sin—our inexcusable, persistent rebellion—against us. He is faithful. We can proclaim, "It is well with my soul!" Then a surge of faith rises up inside of us, and we just want to shout. We just feel like dancing. We just want to put our foot on the devil, for bondage no longer has a hold on us. Whom the Son sets free, is free indeed!

The Holy Spirit completes what He starts. Because part of His job description is to be the "Instigator of Experiential Conviction," He brings it on and carries it through. He never lapses and forgets what He is doing. He never misses a chance to communicate with the ones He reaches out for, and He uses our full range of senses, feelings, and emotions when He convicts us of sin and convinces us of the truth and nothing but the truth.

Even when I feel overwhelmed with deep sorrow and conviction, I say, "Praise the Lord for feelings!" Now, somebody, with feeling, give me a witness!

PRAYER OF A PASSIONATE HEART

Father, I come to You in the fear of the Lord. I receive Your word that tells me, *"Be holy, for I am holy."* I ask You, Holy Spirit, to point out to me the hard places in my heart. Send a revival into my life, my family's life, my church, my community, and my nation. Convict me and all of Your chosen people. Convict us of sin, righteousness, and the judgment to come. Cleanse me from sin. Draw me nearer to You. I want to live my life in a way that is pleasing to You. So, I ask that You would send Your powerful Spirit of conviction upon me and upon those I pray for. Manifest Your holiness and bring me to Yourself. In Jesus's perfect name, amen.

9

Burden-Bearing

"Now Elijah said to Ahab, "Go up, eat and drink; for there is the sound of the roar of a heavy shower." So Ahab went up to eat and drink. But Elijah went up to the top of Carmel; and he crouched down on the earth and put his face between his knees."
—1 Kings 18:41–42

Elijah, what on earth were you doing in this scene? The prophet Elijah's actions were often hard to understand. He took risks and behaved in ways that seemed inappropriate to observers who could not see his internal workings.

The context of the Scripture passage that opens this chapter is a terrible drought. For three and a half years, not a drop of rain had fallen in Israel. The king at the time was wicked Ahab, who could barely tolerate this prophet named Elijah, whom he called the *"troubler of Israel"* (1 Kings 18:17). But he had to listen to him, even if reluctantly, because Elijah got results.

After a mighty demonstration of God's power on the top of Mount Carmel, Elijah had just finished off the prophets of Baal, who were now dead.[28] And he was about to intervene with his prophetic prayers regarding the lack of rain. This was his next assignment from the Lord, and the burden of it felt heavy as soon as the idea settled into his heart. Only God could break the drought and make it rain, and His absolute dominance had just been demonstrated against the 450 pagan prophets of Baal.

Elijah started walking toward Ahab's palace compound. Every step he took raised a little cloud of dust. It was hot, and his sweat made muddy rivulets down his forehead. He approached Ahab's white palace, and his steps slowed as the burden inside him grew. God was going to send rain; of this, he was becoming more and more certain, but he would have to "pray it in" himself.

Elijah was ushered somewhat rudely into the presence of the king. With a distant look in his eyes, Elijah cleared his throat. Internally, his prophetic sense and his faith were growing, even as he opened his mouth to say to Ahab, "*Go up, eat and drink; for there is the sound of the roar of a heavy shower*" (1 Kings 18:41). Ahab was supposed to make ready to celebrate in anticipation of this very good development.

But Elijah himself could not celebrate quite yet. After announcing to King Ahab that rain was on the way, he climbed back up to the top of Mount Carmel, taking his personal servant with him. This was the mountain he had recently descended, the exact spot where he had just performed a tremendous miracle that showed the pagan prophets the power of the God of Israel. So, the top of Mount Carmel was Elijah's place of fresh victory and breakthrough, a perfect place to pray down God's power once again.

How would the Lord do it this time? The breeze was so dry, and Elijah's lips were so parched. But victory was in the air. The burden of the Lord was very real within his heart and mind.

Panting from the exertion of the climb, Elijah found a spot on the dry mountaintop near the charred remains of the spectacular burnt

---

28. The story of Elijah's triumph over the prophets of Baal is told in the same chapter, in 1 Kings 18:20–40.

sacrifice he had lately made. Everything smelled like ashes. He halted, stared at the blackened site, then stepped over to a big outcropping of stone, where he fell to the ground and buried his face between his knees to pray. His servant stood to one side, alert to obey his master's wishes:

> He said to his servant, "Go up now, look toward the sea." So he went up and looked and said, "There is nothing." And he said, "Go back" seven times. It came about at the seventh time, that he said, "Behold, a cloud as small as a man's hand is coming up from the sea." And he said, "Go up, say to Ahab, 'Prepare your chariot and go down, so that the heavy shower does not stop you.'" In a little while the sky grew black with clouds and wind, and there was a heavy shower. And Ahab rode and went to Jezreel. Then the hand of the LORD was on Elijah, and he girded up his loins and outran Ahab to Jezreel.
>
> (1 Kings 18:43–46)

Back and forth the servant traveled between Elijah and his vantage point. Not a cloud could be found in the pale sky. One, two, three, four, five, six times the servant trotted back and forth. Each time, he reported, "Nothing, Master, no clouds at all," and Elijah sent him back to look again. In the meantime, the burden of the Lord settled even more heavily on Elijah. He pressed himself into the earth as if in the travail of childbirth.

Finally, on the seventh time, there was something! *"A cloud as small as a man's hand…,"* the servant reported.

At that, Elijah raised his head. Then he stood up, excited. He dramatically pointed back down the mountain. *"Go up, say to Ahab, 'Prepare your chariot and go down, so that the heavy shower does not stop you.'"* (The king would be going down from his capital in Samaria to his royal residence in Jezreel.) The servant sped off with the message.

Elijah remained on the mountaintop for a moment, gathering strength from the Lord. He felt drained, humble, and utterly dependent on his God. It was as if he had just given birth. He had made the prophetic declaration as clearly as he could. Now it was up to God to make good on the promise of rain. This would not be a light shower, either. It would be a divine *downpour*. Already the tiny cloud appeared larger than before.

Elijah hitched up his robe and sprinted down the mountain toward Ahab's royal residence in Jezreel, about seventeen miles down in the valley. God gave him so much strength that he was able to outrun even the swift chariot of the king, who'd had a head start. It was not raining yet, but once they arrived in Jezreel, the skies opened up. The drought was broken. The word had come to pass.

I must mention the rule that governed prophets in ancient Israel. If a prophetic word did not come to pass, the prophet who had given that word would be stoned to death. This rule put Elijah under a constant threat of death. But even as he prophesied outrageous outcomes, Elijah was never motivated by fear; he was always motivated and directed by the Spirit of God alone, nothing else.

In this case, the parched landscape had mirrored the spiritual landscape of Israel—and then the rain came. Elijah had done his part well.

THIS WOULD NOT BE A LIGHT SHOWER; IT WOULD BE A DIVINE DOWNPOUR.

CARING AND BEARING IN PRAYER

Like a pregnant woman laboring in childbirth, Elijah gave birth to the miracle. Even the position of his body—crouching down with his head low—was similar to the position of a woman in labor in ancient cultures. (Still to this day, women in parts of the world give birth in this position, rather than lying on their backs in a bed.) Elijah had assumed this birthing position, both physically and in his spirit.

The prophet had conceived something by God, and it had grown in his heart. It had become a burden that he simply had to birth. Throughout his travail in prayer, his expectation was sure—there would be rain clouds and a torrent of rain. But he had to pray and pray, sending his servant back and forth to look for the results at regular intervals. His travail expanded the "birth canal" until—behold! A cloud the size of a man's hand! He knew his prayers would succeed.

While bowed down, Elijah was hearing from God's Spirit. He had conceived a vision of rain falling. He had declared, *"There is the sound of the roar of a heavy shower"* (1 Kings 18:41). Then it grew within him. He took steps of action and gave birth to the promise. The drought was ended by heavy rains that came out of nowhere. Heartfelt travail preceded the rain of God's prophetic promise.

We see this kind of prayer again in the New Testament when Paul expresses his parental feelings toward the citizens of the whole region of Galatia. His apostolic burden was to "birth" them in Christ. He could not just pray once for them and wave his hand to claim their salvation and maturation in Christ. He had to *carry* them inside his heart and soul, and it mattered more than anything to him that he be able to carry them successfully to birth: *"My little children, of whom I travail in birth again until Christ be formed in you, I desire to be present with you..."* (Galatians 4:19–20 KJV). In the original Greek, the word *odino*, translated as *"travail in birth,"* means "to feel the pains of child birth," or "to travail."[29]

We find two other Greek words that imply travailing in childbirth in Romans 8:22, where Paul describes how the whole of creation is in a state of travail until the Lord comes at last: *"For we know that the whole creation groaneth and travaileth in pain together until now"* (KJV). The Greek word translated *"groaneth"* is *systenazō*,[30] which means "to moan jointly, i.e. (figurative) experience a common calamity :- groan

29. New Testament Greek Lexicon—King James Version, based on Thayer's and Smith's Bible Dictionary, plus others (public domain), *Strong's* #5605, www.BibleStudyTools.com.
30. Electronic version of *Strong's Exhaustive Concordance of the Bible*, STRONG, (© 1980, 1986, and assigned to World Bible Publishers, Inc. Used by permission. All rights reserved.), #4959.

together." The Greek word for *"travaileth in pain together"* is *synōdinō*[31] (note that one root word of this term is *odino*), which means "(figurative) to sympathize (in expectation of relief from suffering) :- travail in pain together."

A number of Old Testament passages speak directly in terms of "bearing young" in prayer. The Hebrew word that the following passages have in common is *yālad*, among whose meanings are "to bear young; causative to beget; to act as midwife; specifically to show lineage:- bear, beget, birth."[32]

> *Therefore are my loins filled with pain: pangs have taken hold upon me, as the pangs of a woman that **travaileth**: I was bowed down at the hearing of it; I was dismayed at the seeing of it.*
> (Isaiah 21:3 KJV)

> *Be in pain, and labour to bring forth, O daughter of Zion, like a woman in **travail**: for now shalt thou go forth out of the city, and thou shalt dwell in the field, and thou shalt go even to Babylon; there shalt thou be delivered; there the LORD shall redeem thee from the hand of thine enemies.*
> (Micah 4:10 KJV)

> *Therefore will he give them up, until the time that she which **travaileth** hath brought forth: then the remnant of his brethren shall return unto the children of Israel.*
> (Micah 5:3 KJV)

> *Ask ye now, and see whether a man doth travail with child? wherefore do I see every man with his hands on his loins, as a woman in **travail**, and all faces are turned into paleness? Alas! for that day is great, so that none is like it: it is even the time of Jacob's trouble, but he shall be saved out of it.*
> (Jeremiah 30:6–7 KJV)

Although they don't make such a clear connection between travail and prayer, other Old Testament passages use similarly graphic terminology to depict the writhing, almost unbearable pain of childbirth:

---

31. Ibid., #4944.
32. Ibid., #3205.

And they shall be afraid: pangs and sorrows shall take hold of them; they shall be in pain as a woman that travaileth: they shall be amazed one at another; their faces shall be as flames. (Isaiah 13:8 KJV)

Like as a woman with child, that draweth near the time of her delivery, is in pain, and crieth out in her pangs; so have we been in thy sight, O LORD. (Isaiah 26:17 KJV)

PROPHETIC INTERCESSION IS WHEN OUR HEARTS BEAT IN UNION WITH GOD'S HEART.

In citing all of these passages and mentioning the Greek and Hebrew words within them that have to do with the pain of childbirth and the longing for a "child"—the straining and yearning until a certain outcome transpires—I'm trying to make it very clear that the idea of burden-bearing, or travailing, is entirely scriptural. This may help you and others understand what is going on inside. Have you ever felt that you are supposed to carry something in prayer and not stop carrying it, even if it takes a long, long time to see results? Other things you may pray for once only, but not this thing. It burdens you, and you may even groan as if you are in pain.

The birth of a child is one of the most painful and exhausting processes, yet one of the most miraculous and sacred times in a woman's life, truly a time of awe and wonder. And this is the experience that God uses to bless all who care and bear in prayer! This process is often referred to as prophetic intercession. It is when our hearts beat in union with God's heart.[33]

---

33. For more teaching and growth on this strategic subject, see my book *Praying with God's Heart: The Power and the Purpose of Prophetic Intercession* (Minneapolis, MN: Chosen Books, 1999, 2007, 2018).

REAL-LIFE BURDEN-BEARERS

There are many examples of post-biblical intercessory prayers that could be classified as "travail." The following are a few instances that exemplify this form of prayer.

I think of "Praying Hyde" of India. His given name was John Nelson Hyde, and he was an American missionary to northern India in the early part of the twentieth century. A friend who watched him as he prayed for the salvation of the people who lived in the region said, "It was evident to all he was bowed down with sore travail of soul. He missed many meals and when I went to his room, I would find him lying with a great agony, or walking up and down as if an inward fire were burning in his bones."[34] His intense burden was that God would give him a soul a day within that year. He was a burden-bearer for that part of India. By the end of the year, 400 souls had been won to Christ, more than the 365 he had asked for. The next year, he labored in prayer for a goal of two souls a day, and again his request was more than granted—about 800 people came to Christ in that one year. Then he moved the target upward again, to four souls per day for every day of the next year.

Amazingly, in response to Praying Hyde's passionate prayers, his subsequent outreach did not take place in the form of tent crusades or massive rallies. No, he reached out *individually* and personally to one person after another on the village streets. It is said that Hyde would approach sinners on the street of any village at any time, wherever he went. Conversation would ensue, and before long, both he and the villager would kneel in prayer. Hyde would lead the new convert to water and baptize them. He would follow through like this at least four times a day, with complete success that was directly attributable to his prayer-laboring in response to the specific burden the Lord had laid on his spirit. Where would those multitudes of lost souls be today if Praying Hyde had not taken up the prayer burden on their behalf?

---

34. E. G. Carré, *Praying Hyde: Apostle of Prayer* (Alachua, FL: Bridge-Logos, 1982), 28.

And how could I not mention, once again, colonial American David Brainerd, the praying missionary to the indigenous population? His ministry was most fruitful among the Delaware Indians of New Jersey, and it was fruitful because he prayed so much and with such fervor. The following is another excerpt from his journal:

> In prayer I was exceedingly enlarged, and my soul was as much drawn out as ever I remember it to have been in my life, or near. I was in such anguish, and pleaded with so much earnestness and importunity, that when I rose from my knees I felt extremely weak and overcome, I could scarcely walk straight, my joints were loosed, the sweat ran down my face and body, and nature seemed as if it would dissolve. So far as I could judge, I was wholly free from selfish ends in my fervent supplications for the poor Indians. I knew, they were met together to worship devils, and not God; and this made me cry earnestly, that God would now appear, and help me in my attempts to break up this idolatrous meeting. My soul pleaded long....[35]

Do you see what I mean by fervor? Talk about praying with feeling! Brainerd had hold of God's heart for the Delaware Indians, and, letting his heart work in union with God's, he prayed from his heart, the seat of his emotions. It was never a pleasant experience (he writes of "anguish," of being "weak and overcome," having "sweat [run] down [his] face and body," of "nature seem[ing] as if it would dissolve," "cry[ing] earnestly," and his "soul plead[ing] long"). But experiencing pleasant emotions was not the point. Under the tremendous burden of the need for the Indians' salvation, Brainerd allowed his emotions to undergird his prayers to the fullest extent possible. Both Praying Hyde and David Brainerd are classic modern-day examples of prayer burden-bearers.

---

35. Jonathan Edwards, *An Account of the Life of the Late Reverend Mr. David Brainerd, Minister of the Gospel, Missionary to the Indians, from the Honourable Society in Scotland, for the Propagation of Christian Knowledge, and Pastor of a Church of Christian Indians in New-Jersey. Who died at Northampton in New-England, October 9, 1747, in the 30th Year of his Age. Chiefly taken from his own Diary, and other private Writings, written for his own Use; and now published,* journal entry for July 21, 1744 (Edinburgh: John Gray & Gavin Alston, 1765), 123.

Then, close to my heart because I live in "his" city of Franklin, Tennessee, is the Civil War Methodist chaplain E. M. Bounds.[36] In Franklin, he led a prayer revival for three or four years in a church where some of us still carry on annual prayer worship gatherings. Bounds wrote many books about prayer, and the following is a sample of what he said about "importunate prayer":

> The wrestling quality of importunate prayer does not spring from physical vehemence or fleshly energy. It is not an impulse of energy, not mere earnestness of soul; it is an inwrought force, a faculty implanted and aroused by the Holy Spirit. Virtually, it is the intercession of the Holy Spirit of God, in us.[37]

"Importunate prayer" refers, of course, to the story of the "importunate (troublesome and persistent) widow" in Luke 18:1–8, whose burden was receiving a just settlement from a reluctant judge. She made her request so many times, with such fervor, that the judge finally relented and granted her request.

Then there is this story from my own experience of burden-bearing prayer: In 1993, I was leading a group of twenty prophetic intercessors in Herrnhut, Germany. Guided by means of a series of prophetic events, we found our way right into the actual prayer tower that had been used by the Moravians for their day-and-night prayer in the 1700s, which was usually locked. Our purpose was to recover the anointing of those who had participated in that hundred-year-long prayer watch, many of whom were buried nearby in the community cemetery.

As soon as we had climbed the spiral staircase and stepped out onto the top of the tower, looking out over the landscape, the burden of the Lord descended upon us collectively. Unexpectedly, in a split second, we found ourselves in rhythmic travail as one person. We called out in

---

36. Bounds had lived on the north part of the Missouri River in the upper half of the state of Missouri—as did I—and then he moved to Nashville, Tennessee, during the Civil War, after which he moved to Franklin. God moved my family (also in a time of war, the war in Iraq) from Missouri to Nashville and then to Franklin. This connection is very personal to me because I consider Bounds to be a forerunner intercessor who went before me to prepare the way. I know that I walk in his footsteps.

37. E. M. Bounds, *The Necessity of Prayer* (Grand Rapids, MI: Baker, 1979), 63.

strong emotive prayer, which came over us in two waves. The first wave involved calling forth life and the prayer anointing of the past, even as we surveyed the cemetery where many of the legendary Moravians were buried.

Then the second wave came upon all of us; this one was for the prophetic release of this anointing for the "watch of the Lord" like a new Pentecost into 120 specific cities of the world, some of which were represented by the modern-day intercessors in the "upper room" where we were praying. This was a forerunner activity, as it occurred before houses of prayer had been established, for the most part. Since then, houses of prayer have sprung up worldwide, many in the exact cities we prayed for that day. We see this modern-day "watch of the Lord" as a direct answer to our travailing prayer.

BURDEN-BEARING FROM AN EMOTIONAL PERSPECTIVE

All of this burden-bearing and travailing involves...guess what? Emotions and feelings—lots of them.

This rather emotive, Feeler form of intercessory prayer may involve every part of a believer's being—spirit, soul, and body—with a special emphasis on the heart as the seat of the emotions. Wesley Duewel gives us these insights in his book *Mighty Prevailing Prayer*: "A prayer burden is a spiritual concern on the heart of God that is imparted by the Holy Spirit to someone whose intercession the Holy Spirit desires to use.... It is a specially sacred level of prayer intensity and prayer responsibility."[38]

Burden-bearing is another way of sensing, discerning, or knowing the voice of the Holy Spirit, and it has occurred throughout Jewish and Christian history. The senses involved can range from gentle nudging of thoughts to gut-wrenching weeping and travail of heart and soul.

When God is easing a prayer burden onto you, it may start tenderly with gentle sensations. It increases gradually to the point of feeling

---

38. Wesley L. Duewel, *Mighty Prevailing Prayer* (Grand Rapids, MI.: Zondervan, 1990), 200.

like the wrenching pains of childbirth or a volcanic eruption inside. The presence or glory of God—the *kabowd*, in Hebrew[39]—is weighty by definition, and the weight increases as a person responds to it. You might see the following stages of development if God wants you to pray in this manner:

+ You begin to sense a spiritual concern. This concern is granted by God; it is not something that you conjure up on your own.

+ The concern develops into a prayer burden, and it becomes very personal and heartfelt.

+ You may become aware that this is a sacred trust when you find yourself carrying this growing concern as a mother carries a child forming inside her during pregnancy.

+ You will need to sustain your focus until the promise can be birthed. You may well need the support of others to be able to carry the burden, even enlisting others in this intercessory task.

+ You may experience a purging fire of the Holy Spirit during the time you carry the prayer burden.

+ Finally, release will occur when the promised result comes to pass (or when you receive an assurance that God has already answered in the spiritual realm and the manifestation will soon appear). You will have a sense of relief and overwhelming joy as the plans, purposes, and destiny of God manifest themselves in the natural realm.

As a Feeler, you should know how important your senses are to this kind of prayer. Without your sanctified senses, you can't pick up on the first hint of a prayer burden, let alone carry it all the way, through thick and thin, to the completion of your assignment. I have included this chapter of teaching about intercessory prayer because your entire emotional capacity gets engaged in this kind of prayer. When a burden of the Lord is transferred into your heart (and gut), you become a "Feeler Burden-Bearer."

---

39. *Strong's* #3519.

> *BURDEN-BEARING IS ANOTHER WAY OF SENSING, DISCERNING, OR KNOWING THE VOICE OF THE HOLY SPIRIT. THE SENSES INVOLVED CAN RANGE FROM GENTLE NUDGING OF THOUGHTS TO GUT-WRENCHING WEEPING AND TRAVAIL OF HEART AND SOUL.*

HIS BURDEN IS EASY

Too many Feeler-intercessors carry the burden for too long, though. When they do that, it bears them down and wears them down. Remember that a prayer burden comes from God, and you are supposed to carry your share of it only until you can return it to God with your task accomplished. You are never meant to carry it forever. Jesus tells you, *"Take My yoke upon you and learn from Me, for I am gentle and lowly in heart, and you will find rest for your souls. For My yoke is easy and My burden is light"* (Matthew 11:29–30 NKJV). When you are yoked with Jesus, He is carrying most of the burden on His strong shoulders; He needs you only to share it with Him, not take it all upon yourself.

Just as all four of the gospels record how Jesus used a young donkey to carry Him into Jerusalem, in a similar way, you and I may be called to become "jackasses for Jesus" (no offense intended). The donkey was and is a beast of burden, and Jesus selected that particular animal to be His carrier for a short journey into Jerusalem. When He selects one of us to be His burden-carrier for a time, we need to be willing to bear up under the load and travel where He directs us to go. We can be carriers of His divine purposes by being Feeler-intercessors.

The destination of your journey is the throne of God, where you will deposit your assigned burden before the Father. Remember—and this word to the wise comes from years of personal experience—pick up only what is your assignment from God. Carry it by His grace, and then give it back to Him. Be a happy burden-bearer, even if the weight is almost too much for you. Don't be a heavy-laden intercessor. *"For this is the love of God, that we keep His commandments. And His commandments are not burdensome"* (1 John 5:3 NKJV).

Like that beast of burden that carried Jesus the Messiah to His appointment in Jerusalem, consider it a great honor for the cargo of God to come and rest or sit upon you. Just remember, your job is to carry this burden to the throne on behalf of another and then let it go. Pick it up and let it go. That's what we Feeler prayer warriors do! We pick it up, carry it for a distance, and then let it go to the throne of the almighty God!

PRAYER OF A PASSIONATE HEART

Holy God, I exalt Your majestic name! I count it an honor to be a beast of burden to carry Your plans, purposes, and pursuits. I am so grateful that You would trust me with Your heart and that You want me to know how You feel about a given situation. Grant me greater grace to effectively discern these ancient ways and see them restored to the body of Christ in this day. I surrender to You to be a burden-bearer, in Jesus's magnificent name. Amen and amen!

10

Discerning Atmospheres

"And an angel of the Lord suddenly stood before them,
and the glory of the Lord shone around them;
and they were terribly frightened."
—Luke 2:9

Our goal as followers of Jesus is to have a relationship with the Father, just as Jesus has. Like Him, we want to "do what the Father is doing." When Jesus walked on the earth, He said, *"Very truly I tell you, the Son can do nothing by himself; he can do only what he sees his Father doing, because whatever the Father does the Son also does"* (John 5:19 NIV).

But how on earth can you tell what Jesus and the Father are doing? It isn't easy, is it? You may be thinking, "I'm not God, as Jesus is. How can I expect to know what the Father is doing?" But remember, the Holy Spirit, the third person of the Trinity, dwells inside you. He will help you discern what God is doing and will show you how to take part in it. He will also help you discern the invisible interference that may surround you at times. With the help of the Holy Spirit, you can discern the spiritual atmosphere wherever you go.

FOLLOW HIM WHEREVER HE LEADS

God has always made sure that His people had a way of discerning where He was going so that they might follow Him accurately. At the time of the exodus, He led the Israelites through the wilderness by sending physical signals in the form of "pillars" of cloud or fire: *"The Lord guided them by a pillar of cloud during the daytime and by a pillar of fire at night. So they could travel either by day or night"* (Exodus 13:21 TLB). Throughout the Old Testament, God guided His people both individually and corporately.

When Jesus was born in Bethlehem, the unsuspecting shepherds were startled when *"an angel of the Lord suddenly stood before them, and the glory of the Lord shone around them"* (Luke 2:9). Then the angel told them about the holy birth in the nearby town so they would go to investigate and later testify about what they had seen that night.

After His resurrection, Jesus sent His Holy Spirit to His disciples, having told them, *"The fact of the matter is that it is best for you that I go away, for if I don't, the Comforter won't come. If I do, he will—for I will send him to you"* (John 16:7 TLB). Having the Comforter (the Holy Spirit) dwelling inside them made it possible for believers to "live in the light" all the time and to be alert to encroaching darkness so they could dispel it in Jesus's name. Paul wrote to the church in Ephesus, which was surrounded with much darkness in the form of pagan worship and sinful living: *"For you were once darkness, but now you are light in the Lord. Live as children of light (for the fruit of the light consists in all goodness, righteousness and truth) and **find out what pleases the Lord**"* (Ephesians 5:8–10 NIV).

Practically speaking, how can you "find out what pleases the Lord" so that you can follow Him more closely? How can you follow closely enough to "live as a child of light"? Asking yourself these four simple questions may help you feel your way through the discernment process:

1. What are Jesus and the Father doing in this situation?

2. What is the Holy Spirit doing?

3. Is there an atmosphere of faith and expectation?

4. Is there a presence of doubt and unbelief?

Of course, you will almost never get the answer to the first two questions in the form of an audible word from heaven, but you should begin to be able to discern what God is doing—and whether you are supposed to participate in some way—by answering the other two questions.

The third question ("Is there an atmosphere of faith and expectation?") brings us into the meat of this chapter—how *can* you distinguish one "atmosphere" from another? How can you tell the difference between, for example, "getting up on the wrong side of the bed" and sensing an unpleasant, evil influence in your environment? How can you determine the origin of an atmosphere that seems to be filled with expectation? Is it from human hype or the Holy Spirit?

> **KNOWING WHAT PLEASES THE LORD STARTS WITH AN ABILITY TO PERCEIVE GOD'S PRESENCE AND OTHER SUPERNATURAL PRESENCES.**

DISCERNING THE TANGIBLE PRESENCE

Knowing what pleases the Lord starts with an ability to perceive God's presence and other supernatural presences. Throughout the Old and New Testaments, we see written evidence of instances where biblical figures—who, remember, were people just like us—discerned that God was tangibly present, a reality that increased their faith and awareness of potential marvels. We also see instances where God's people discerned that a demonic influence was present. Finally, we notice that biblical characters did not always immediately perceive the nature of the spiritual atmospheres around them. They had to learn to do this, just as we do. All the senses are involved in such discernment. The following is a sampling of biblical figures who experienced supernatural encounters:

Moses: *"Then Moses said, 'Now show me your glory.' And the* LORD *said, "I will cause all my goodness to pass in front of you, and I will proclaim my name, the* LORD, *in your presence"* (Exodus 33:18–19 NIV).

David: *"The one thing I want from God, the thing I seek most of all, is the privilege of meditating in his Temple, living in his presence every day of my life, delighting in his incomparable perfections and glory"* (Psalm 27:4 TLB).

Ezekiel: *"Then the man brought me by way of the north gate to the front of the temple. I looked and saw the glory of the* LORD *filling the temple of the* LORD, *and I fell facedown"* (Ezekiel 44:4 NIV).

Zechariah: *"Then an angel of the Lord appeared to him, standing at the right side of the altar of incense. When Zechariah saw him, he was startled and was gripped with fear. But the angel said to him: 'Do not be afraid, Zechariah; your prayer has been heard. Your wife Elizabeth will bear you a son, and you are to call him John. He will be a joy and delight to you, and many will rejoice because of his birth, for he will be great in the sight of the Lord. He is never to take wine or other fermented drink, and he will be filled with the Holy Spirit even before he is born. He will bring back many of the people of Israel to the Lord their God. And he will go on before the Lord, in the spirit and power of Elijah, to turn the hearts of the parents to their children and the disobedient to the wisdom of the righteous—to make ready a people prepared for the Lord.'"* (Luke 1:11–17 NIV)

Jesus's disciples: *"When the disciples saw Him walking on the sea, they were terrified, and said, 'It is a ghost!' And they cried out in fear. But immediately Jesus spoke to them, saying, 'Take courage, it is I; do not be afraid'"* (Matthew 14:26–27).

Paul: *"Once when we were going to the place of prayer, we were met by a female slave who had a spirit by which she predicted the future. She earned a great deal of money for her owners by fortune-telling.*

She followed Paul and the rest of us, shouting, 'These men are servants of the Most High God, who are telling you the way to be saved.' She kept this up for many days. Finally Paul became so annoyed that he turned around and said to the spirit, 'In the name of Jesus Christ I command you to come out of her!' At that moment the spirit left her" (Acts 16:16–18 NIV).

John: *"I, John, your brother and companion in the suffering and kingdom and patient endurance that are ours in Jesus, was on the island of Patmos because of the word of God and the testimony of Jesus. On the Lord's Day I was in the Spirit, and I heard behind me a loud voice like a trumpet, which said: 'Write on a scroll what you see and send it to the seven churches: to Ephesus, Smyrna, Pergamum, Thyatira, Sardis, Philadelphia and Laodicea.' I turned around to see the voice that was speaking to me. And when I turned I saw seven golden lampstands, and among the lampstands was someone like a son of man, dressed in a robe reaching down to his feet and with a golden sash around his chest. The hair on his head was white like wool, as white as snow, and his eyes were like blazing fire. His feet were like bronze glowing in a furnace, and his voice was like the sound of rushing waters"* (Revelation 1:9–15 NIV).

In most of these cases, the atmosphere being discerned was a heavenly one. Yes, when heaven invades earth, we see responses of worship, awe, wonder, delight.

The story about the disciples in the boat illustrates their complete *inability* to discern the presence of the Lord in the midst of their own terror. And when we read about Paul being hounded by the slave who had a spirit of divination, we learn that his very irritation turned out to be the best evidence that the atmosphere she carried with her was an evil one. It seems to have taken him several days to figure that out. He could feel the smothering atmosphere whenever she came onto the scene, but he had to discern it by degrees as the days went on. He did not jump on it immediately. At first, he may not have understood the reason for his persistent annoyance. At last, his aggravation increased to the point that he knew what to do, and he cast the spirit of divination out of the woman.

You and I are unlikely to find ourselves in a storm-tossed boat, watching Jesus approach us walking on top of the waves. Nor will many of us ever be trailed by an evil-spirit-controlled slave. However, we need to learn from such accounts how to appropriately respond to the spiritual atmosphere around us. Most of the time, things will be quiet and appear normal—there will be neither an identifiably heavenly presence nor an evil one. But from time to time, we will be thrust into situations where we need to use all of our senses to discern the spiritual atmosphere. You can't really learn what to do and how to properly do it from books alone—although it is my goal that this book will assist you in sharpening your senses and in knowing what to pay attention to as we navigate this complex world of feelings.

In my own experience, discerning the presence of heavenly angels, their demonic counterparts, and specific evil principalities has sometimes been a "crash course." For example, years ago, my wife and I experienced nine straight weeks of angelic encounters from midnight until five o'clock in the morning. Our humble home was a place of heavenly visitation, week after week, and no two nights were the same. (Even so, we probably experienced only a sampling of the many heavenly realms.) Most of the time, it was absolutely overwhelming.

Sometimes, we were overcome with the fear of the Lord; sometimes, we were crushingly aware of the destiny of God; sometimes, we were swept up in worshipful awe and wonder. There is no way we could have invented any of it out of our imaginations because these heavenly encounters so far exceeded anything we had ever even heard of.

The nine straight weeks of visitations were prophesied, in part, to me ahead of time by the seer-prophet Bob Jones. These and other close encounters of a heavenly kind are well documented in many of my books cowritten with Michal Ann, such as *Angelic Encounters*, *The Call to Courage*, and *God Encounters Today*. Our experiences influenced us as we selected a name for our ministry, God Encounters Ministries.

During that time of visitation, we began to learn the distinctions between various kinds of angels. It makes sense that angels would have been created to "specialize" in revealing specific aspects of the nature of God; since God is higher, deeper, wider, and bigger than anything, anywhere, He needs a whole host of heavenly beings to reveal all the facets of His glory to mortals such as us.

For example, I now know of personal guardian angels, other angels of protection, divine watchers, angels who have oversight of regions and nations, warrior angels, messenger angels, angels who release God's healing anointing, the fiery seraphim, angels who appear as winds of change, and angels who escort our saved souls to heaven. Those are just a few of the different categories of angels who serve God in special ways.

With a certain amount of experience and with the help of the Holy Spirit, you, too, can learn not only to discern the atmosphere of heaven that angels bring when they come, but also the intents and purposes of angels. In other words, angels come to show us what to do, whether it is worshipping, praying, or reaching out in a particular way. As a Feeler, or as a Spirit-filled believer in Christ Jesus, you can grow in your discernment to detect which category of angel is present and how to work with them.

WITH A CERTAIN AMOUNT OF EXPERIENCE AND WITH THE HELP OF THE HOLY SPIRIT, YOU, TOO, CAN LEARN NOT ONLY TO DISCERN THE ATMOSPHERE OF HEAVEN THAT ANGELS BRING WHEN THEY COME, BUT ALSO THE INTENTS AND PURPOSES OF ANGELS.

You may also have other experiences. The Holy Spirit may come with the unmistakable fire of His presence, bringing not only warmth but also comfort, healing, and deliverance. You may have a visitation from an individual, either an actual person or a vision of that person. Once, John Wimber appeared to me in an open vision and made an announcement, "It's the beginning of the fourth wave," whereupon the atmosphere of the room became saturated with the unmistakable atmosphere of heavenly destiny. This was a declaration that another move of the Holy Spirit was coming to the body of Christ and would come crashing in upon the shores of time.[40]

You may even go into a spiritual trance, as the apostle Peter did when he was staying in the home of Simon the tanner, and the Spirit wanted him (even though he was an observant Jew) to go to the house of the "unclean" Gentile Roman military officer, Cornelius. (See Acts 10.) Apparently, this was the best way to persuade Peter to do something that he never would have chosen to do otherwise.

This is not exactly the same experience, but, not long ago, something like that happened to me when I was on the verge of kidney failure, with two other organs already having shut down. I was lying in my bed when my spirit was taken to heaven. There, I saw my parents, my late wife, and others who had graduated to their eternal, heavenly reward. Everything and everyone looked so vibrant and beautiful, and I felt so whole and healthy.

Then a heavenly messenger passed through a translucent veil while I was still in heaven and was now speaking to me from my own bedroom back on earth. This messenger told me, "You must stay on this side [there on earth]. Your job on this side is not yet complete. You must stay on this side." Those words shocked me into action, and my spirit flew back from heaven and hit my body in the bed. My bedroom was totally filled with wondrous awe. I had been given a fresh commission, along with the faith to fulfill it—and my organ failure was reversed as well.

---

40. The late John Wimber was known as the leader of the "Third Wave" movement in the modern church.

All heavenly encounters bring with them the supercharged atmosphere of heaven. You can't help but be awed by a sense of God's holiness, as new faith surges up from within. In the Feeler realm, we can discern external spiritual atmospheres, and I believe that various forms of "God encounters" will be on the increase in the lives of ordinary believers as the last days approach.

DISCERNING ATMOSPHERES

A large part of discerning atmospheres is distinguishing the presence of different categories of spirits. I think of Hebrews 5:14: *"But solid food is for the mature, who because of practice have their senses trained to discern good and evil."*

Such heavenly encounters as the ones just described help to throw *un*heavenly encounters into sharper relief. Discerning atmospheres includes discerning the presence of dark spirits. Sometimes, your senses will pick up only subtle clues; other times, the atmosphere will be unquestionably evil. The following is an account of a dramatic experience that happened to me.

Once, in the middle of the night, I was alone in the bedroom of our farmhouse when the air turned ice-cold. I woke up to find that the temperature had plummeted something like thirty degrees. No windows had been opened, and it wasn't that cold outside, anyway. I knew the room had been dialed down to an unnatural temperature for an unnatural reason. Then a figure who looked like Darth Vader from *Star Wars*, wrapped in gold chains, appeared in the room.

I was kind of paralyzed, knowing but not really knowing what was going on. This personage appeared to be exuding a spirit of death. I struggled to say the name of Jesus: "Je...Je...Je...." Eventually, I spoke the entire name, "Jesus." Instantly, the dark apparition disappeared, and the coldness vanished with it. The room returned to a normal temperature, and the atmosphere was now charged with faith instead of foreboding fear. This was not just a personal or family spiritual battle I was engaged in. Because I am an ambassador of the Lord on behalf of my assigned sphere of jurisdiction, I knew this was a regional issue dealing with territorial demonic spirits.

Another time, I was ministering in South Central Europe in what was then known as Yugoslavia. I was assisting Mahesh Chavda, who was leading the evening crusade gatherings. He had prayed for some people, and one young man was lying on the floor afterward, immobilized—and turning blue with cold. I was trying to pick up on the spiritual atmosphere because, clearly, something was going on. I felt the presence of what I would term a death culture coming from an evil spirit, and I knew that it was hindering this young man. Suddenly, the man, who did not speak English, said, in English, "Take the book. Take the book out."

I somehow knew what to do next. I turned to my interpreter and said, "Flip him over." When we turned his body over, I saw a copy of *Mein Kampf*, Adolf Hitler's fascist manifesto, sticking out of his hip pocket. We pulled it out of his pocket, and the whole spiritual atmosphere shifted. The man sat up and experienced instantaneous deliverance. In the next moments, he was saved and baptized in the Holy Spirit, and then he began speaking in tongues. Exhilarated, he said, through the interpreter, "Your Jesus makes me higher than any drug I've ever taken."

MY FATHER'S HOUSE HAS MANY ROOMS

At the end of the Last Supper, after Judas had gone out and Jesus's disciples were very sad, Jesus comforted them, saying,

Do not let your heart be troubled; believe in God, believe also in Me. In My Father's house are many dwelling places; if it were not so, I would have told you; for I go to prepare a place for you. If I go and prepare a place for you, I will come again and receive you to Myself, that where I am, there you may be also.   (John 14:1–3)

In our Father's heavenly house are many dwelling places, and we ourselves are each a dwelling place for the Spirit of the Father. Each dwelling place carries a certain atmosphere.

Just stop and think about the way houses "feel different" from each other inside. And think about the various rooms of a house in terms of how they *feel*. Each house, and every room in a house, has a distinct atmosphere. A kitchen feels quite different from a basement. A bedroom feels different from a front porch. So it is anywhere you go. Thus, you may be walking down the street, prayer-walking or just silently conversing with the Lord, and you can sense the spiritual atmosphere emanating from a particular building or location. However, you can't discern the atmosphere if you are distracted; you have to be intentionally paying attention to what the Holy Spirit may be showing you.

IN OUR FATHER'S HEAVENLY HOUSE ARE MANY DWELLING PLACES, AND WE OURSELVES ARE EACH A DWELLING PLACE FOR THE SPIRIT OF THE FATHER. EACH DWELLING PLACE CARRIES A CERTAIN ATMOSPHERE.

As mentioned in chapter 7, the late prophet Bob Jones was amazingly gifted when it came to discerning atmospheres. When he would feel wind blowing indoors, he would ask, "Did you feel the wind blowing on that?" It indicated to him that angels were present in the place. Other times, he would feel fire, which was connected with healing. His arms would grow cold in the presence of demonic activity. He was also able to sense, feel, and know locations over which there were "open heavens," and he could take prayerful action accordingly.

It makes me think of *The Interior Castle*, written in the 1500s by St. Teresa of Avila, a Spanish Carmelite nun. The work describes a series of heavenly rooms, each of which contained new revelations and atmospheres. Some were dazzling, and some were filled with peace, while others were filled with the fear of the Lord. No two rooms were the same, and each room called forth a certain response.

Paul Cox, whose California ministry is called Aslan's Place, is the most advanced "Feeler-prophet" I know. In his life of ministry, Paul has been taken in the Spirit to visit various rooms in the Father's house. He found that each one is filled with a distinct purpose and a sense of destiny. For example, he reports visiting the Father's throne room, His war room, His map room, and His waiting room. He has viewed rooms filled with various body parts (for healing purposes) and a garden of His delights. One room is stocked with divine revelations, another with fragrances.

Other rooms Paul saw include God's library, His "recovery room," an armory, a council room, a "cupbearer room," an Esther room, a seer room, and a scroll room, as well as rooms dedicated to worship, equipping, rest, strategies, inventions, promises, travail, and the glory of God.[41] When he visited each one of those rooms, Paul could sense a different atmosphere. Every room has a special purpose and carries a distinct scent, presence, even an aroma of the Lord.

My friend and mentor Mahesh Chavda is very sensitive to the emotions and activity of the Holy Spirit. He is like a weather vane; when he feels the presence of God, he turns as God wishes. He operates by sensing the spiritual atmosphere around him, and he can shift the atmosphere of a place from doubt to faith or from iniquity to mercy. He not only can sense an atmosphere of anointing, but he can also transmit the supernatural enablement of grace to others.

FLESHING IT OUT

How does all this relate to you? I'm putting into words certain experiences that demonstrate the existence of the Seer and Feeler realms. Whether by faith or by ascending in worship and then entering into an encounter with the Holy Spirit, any of us can sense a surge of supernatural faith or feel an anointing for healing. Angels can take people into

41. For more, see Paul L. Cox, *Heaven Trek* (Apple Valley, CA: Aslan's Place, 2007).

various places that, at times, can look like rooms, to provide heavenly solutions. All things are possible in God.

I can think of a number of ways that people express what they are sensing when they are picking up on a spiritual atmosphere:

- "It feels like there's a brass ceiling for some reason."
- "I feel sad for some reason."
- "I sense there's a deep disappointment that the Holy Spirit wants to heal."
- "It feels like this region has missed a move of God."
- "It feels like things are stuck in the past here."
- "When I crossed the county line, I felt that heaviness lift."
- "Where's that wind coming from? Did you feel that?"
- "A new day is coming. I know it! I feel it. Things are changing!"
- "Did you feel the shift? Things are about to break open."

Once you know something about such senses and different levels of discernment, you can pay attention to your own senses, and you will be better able to learn your own personal "Feeler language," or what your various senses mean. This will aid in your intercession and your deliverance or healing ministry. It will equip you for involvement in spiritual warfare.

FORERUNNERS AND EQUIPPERS

My late wife, Michal Ann, had an amazing ability to discern and shift atmospheres. She was a doorkeeper in the house of the Lord with a "breaker anointing," often going into prayers of travail and groaning until she could identify demonic resistance and then pushing right through it. When she discerned a place that was spiritually dull or dry, she would call for the rain of the Holy Spirit—and it would fall. She especially had authority to break the deaf and dumb spirit off of people and regions.

The late Jill Austin, founder of Master Potter Ministries, was one of the most amazing movers in the Holy Spirit I have ever witnessed in my lifetime. When she said, "Fire!" fire fell, and you could tangibly feel it! Not only were individuals deeply touched, but entire rooms and auditoriums of people would be overwhelmed by the raw fire of God. She indeed was a forerunner who blazed a trail that others would learn to follow in her updraft. She, too, is looking down on us today from heaven's balcony, cheering us on.

God always has His forerunners, and He also has equippers—men and women who can discern atmospheres and also discern what to do about what they have discerned. They model for us a way of operating. God uses them to displace doubt and unbelief.

Paul Cox not only can feel out atmospheres and be sensitive to the divine directives, but he also is sensitive enough to discern how far out the influence of a demonic spirit emanates. Additionally, he can sense the relative "weightiness" of a spiritual gift that a person carries. He knows whether a person is highly gifted or only touched lightly with a gift, and he often knows the relative level of spiritual authority that a person carries. Again, I esteem Paul Cox as a General in the Faith in the prophetic Feeler realm.

GOD ALWAYS HAS HIS FORERUNNERS, AND HE ALSO HAS EQUIPPERS—MEN AND WOMEN WHO CAN DISCERN ATMOSPHERES AND ALSO DISCERN WHAT TO DO ABOUT WHAT THEY HAVE DISCERNED.

Jesus Himself, of course, could easily discern atmospheres—and cause them to change. He could tell when people were not ready for His message, or when they were rebellious or dishonest. He could see the intentions of their hearts, for good or for bad. He could see above the storm clouds and speak peace to the actual atmosphere, making the tempests die down. He knew when His time came to be crucified, so that, resolutely, He could present Himself to fulfill the Father's will.

Many people find that they not only can discern the difference between demonic and divine spirits, but also the spirit that someone is "in" at the moment. For example, they might be able to tell that a person has been assigned to carry darkness into a situation or region. (This might not be the same as that person being demonized.) On the positive side, they might know that someone is carrying a spirit of peace that could quell a conflict. The sensitive Feeler-Discerner might be aware of when and how another believer could carry the atmosphere of an open heaven into a situation that needs an especially strong touch from God, or the timing of when a fellow follower of Christ should act to dislodge a dark demonic power and release the opposite spirit.

You, too, can learn to discern atmospheres and to be a carrier of God's divine presence. To do so, you must determine to wait on the Lord expectantly. Lean in toward Him. Seek His face. Soak in His presence. Worship Him.

REST AROUND THE ARK

Would you like a key to shifting the atmosphere in your home? Do you need some help discerning the predominant spirit at work in your region? I have a key for you from the life of a child—the life of the boy Samuel: it is to rest near the ark of God's covenantal presence.

Samuel had been dedicated to the Lord as a baby and was growing up in the temple. I am sure he had his own bedroom, but we find him resting around the ark of the covenant. While he was resting there, the Spirit of God called out to him three times, and each time he thought it must be the old priest Eli summoning him. Then, after the fourth time, he got up and said, *"Speak, for Your servant is listening"* (1 Samuel 3:10).

At that point, Samuel had entered into the atmosphere of the Lord's presence. He learned to discern the voice of God from the voice of a man. God's voice was amplified, and secrets began to be shared with the servant of the Lord. (You can read the whole story in 1 Samuel 3:1–19.)

The key? Rest around the ark of God. The key? God speaks where He dwells. Want to hear His voice? Then be in His presence! Want to discern and shift atmospheres? Learn the atmosphere of heaven!

Let's not just talk about it. Come with me into His presence right now! Let's start by praying once again.

PRAYER OF A PASSIONATE HEART

Heavenly Father, I come to You in the majestic name of the Lord Jesus Christ. I want to be a doorkeeper in the house of the Lord and discern Your every motion. Teach me to discern the true from the false, the holy from the profane, the genuine from the deceptive, and the angelic from the demonic. I pray to see open heavens over my days and to usher in open heavens for others; I volunteer to be Your fire-carrier. Letting my faith rise up, I declare that a new breed of discerners is emerging, and I'm part of it by stepping forward. I want to bring breakthrough wherever I go. Greater are You in me than he who is in the world, dear Lord! Amen.

11

Wisdom for Feelers

"Blessed are those who find wisdom,
those who gain understanding."
—Proverbs 3:13 (NIV)

Regarding the Feeler realm, I'm aware that much of this material has seldom been explored in depth. I feel like a pioneer or a trailblazer surveying new territory. Delving into the ins and outs of being a Feeler reminds me that one of the areas trailblazers are often weak in is *wisdom*. After all, trailblazers keep their eyes looking ahead. They do not tend to worry about incidentals. They press on toward their goal without concerning themselves about explaining everything, disregarding their own comfort—and, likewise, the comfort of those who follow after them. The important thing is getting there, not keeping track of every slippery place.

With that in mind, it's time to address the need for Feelers to act with circumspection, wisdom, and integrity. Because I have been called to the office of prophet with a ministry of teaching (mostly about topics pertaining to the prophetic, prayer, and the presence of God), I am acutely aware of my need for wisdom—God's wisdom—every single day.

In this chapter, I turn our attention to the wisdom needs of Feelers, who, as we know, operate largely out of their emotions. Yet none of us, even those who are more cerebral, start out wise. Each person must learn wisdom along the way, and we must learn to value the lessons of wisdom, as well, even as those sometimes come to us the "hard way." We must be hungry for the wisdom of God and aware of our need for it.

If we want to finish well after long, fruitful lives and ministries, we must attend to three strands of life in particular: (1) fullness of character, (2) fullness of power, and (3) fullness of God's wisdom. These three aspects are woven together like the unbreakable three-strand cord referred to by wise King Solomon in one of his life lessons from the book of Ecclesiastes: *"A cord of three strands is not quickly broken"* (Ecclesiastes 4:12 NIV).

FULLNESS OF CHARACTER

Character is of utmost importance, and God created us to reflect His character. Fullness of character is exemplified by the fruit of the Spirit, which is, again, *"love, joy, peace, patience, kindness, goodness, faithfulness, gentleness, self-control"* (Galatians 5:22–23). Each element matters, and, as Paul states in 1 Corinthians 13:13, love is the most important of all. Feelers who lack love, joy, peace, patience, kindness, goodness, faithfulness, gentleness, and self-control will be a burden on their fellow believers and on others.

Foundational to your life as a follower of Christ Jesus is taking up your cross on a daily basis. Jesus made this fact very clear when He said, *"If anyone desires to come after Me, let him deny himself, and take up his cross daily, and follow Me"* (Luke 9:23 NKJV). This means walking alongside Jesus every day, every step of the way. If you ask Him, He will help you, and He will fill out your character in the process.

By the way, when we lift high the standard of God's Word, encouraging believers to pick up their cross daily and die to self, we are reaffirming sound, apostolic New Testament teaching. The bottom line: having a healthy character contributes greatly to the development of true wisdom.

FULLNESS OF POWER

The fullness of character could be called the new wineskin that can be filled with new wine. (See, for example, Matthew 9:17.) Being filled with new wine means being endued with new power. When you have developed good character and are receiving a steady supply of divine power, the Holy Spirit can use you well, and your gifts can bear good fruit: *"God always has shown us that these messages are true by signs and wonders and various miracles and by giving certain special abilities from the Holy Spirit to those who believe; yes, God has assigned such gifts to each of us"* (Hebrews 2:4 TLB). Filled with His power, you can use whatever gifts He has given you, and the people around you will benefit. (See, for example, 1 Peter 4:10–11.)

Wisdom dictates that when you reach out with *God's* power, you are not building up your own platform but rather building up the people He puts around you. A key to increase is to do something with what you already possess. If you do nothing with what you have, you will have only what you currently possess. If you give away what you have, it will multiply. It will not only multiply through others, but it will also multiply in and through you. This is the way the kingdom of God works! It is the kingdom way of increase in revelation and in vocal and power gifts. Give, and it shall be given! (See Luke 6:38.)

WISDOM DICTATES THAT WHEN YOU REACH OUT WITH GOD'S POWER, YOU ARE NOT BUILDING UP YOUR OWN PLATFORM BUT RATHER BUILDING UP THE PEOPLE HE PUTS AROUND YOU.

FULLNESS OF GOD'S WISDOM

Wisdom is essential for operating in the Feeler realm, and not just any wisdom. We need to enter into the fullness of God's wisdom, in particular, and I want to lead you to seek that wisdom. It would be easy for me to say, "Just get wisdom." In fact, that's what we are urged to do in the book of Proverbs: *"The beginning of wisdom is this: Get wisdom. Though it cost all you have, get understanding"* (Proverbs 4:7 NIV). But how can you "get" wisdom?

The world around you offers a multitude of sources for wisdom. "Buy this product!" "Visit this place!" "Try this exercise!" "Take this class!" But the wisdom of the world comes from human sources or, many times, from darker sources, whereas the wisdom we need most comes straight from God Himself. You can tell the difference between worldly wisdom and divine, heavenly wisdom by the results in a person's life: *"The wisdom that is from above is first pure, then peaceable, gentle, willing to yield, full of mercy and good fruits, without partiality and without hypocrisy"* (James 3:17 NKJV).

HOW TO ACQUIRE WISDOM

How can you obtain this godly wisdom? *Pray* for it—and not just once in a while. Amazingly, when I was just a boy in rural Missouri, God had me praying over and over for the wisdom I didn't really know I would need. I grew up in a family that hardly knew the Bible, and yet God dropped several specific prayers into my heart, and this was one of them: "Lord, give me wisdom beyond my years, like Solomon." (See 2 Chronicles 1:7–12.) I prayed that special prayer for years. Now, I doubt I'll ever approach the phenomenal wisdom of Solomon, but I do know that God was his *Source* of wisdom, as He has been my Source as well. I continue to pray for wisdom as often as I can. May the Lord remind me of its importance, morning, noon, and night!

Thus, we need to start by praying for wisdom. "Lord, give me wisdom" must be our request, because wisdom will not be given to us automatically—and even if it were, I don't think we would value it as wisdom without God's help.

We read the words of James, apostle and brother of Jesus, who wrote simply, *"If any of you lacks wisdom, let him ask of God, who gives to all generously and without reproach, and it will be given to him"* (James 1:5). Notice that it says, *"If any of you lacks wisdom…."* That phrase shows us that we must recognize our lack of wisdom. Then, humbly, we open ourselves to receive what we need.

It helps also to acknowledge God's fullness of supply; He is all-wise and all-sufficient and ever willing to dispense whatever we lack. The following is exactly what Solomon did when he was elevated to the throne of Israel and saw clearly how lacking in wisdom he was:

> *Solomon said to God, "You have dealt with my father David with great lovingkindness, and have made me king in his place. Now, O LORD God, Your promise to my father David is fulfilled, for You have made me king over a people as numerous as the dust of the earth. Give me now wisdom and knowledge, that I may go out and come in before this people, for who can rule this great people of Yours?"* (2 Chronicles 1:8–10)

In asking God for His gift of wisdom, we are asking for more of God Himself. He is the Source of all true wisdom: *"The fear of the LORD is the beginning of wisdom; all who follow his precepts have good understanding. To him belongs eternal praise"* (Psalm 111:10 NIV). Notice the last part—*"to him belongs eternal praise"*—because when you draw wisdom from the Source, you give glory to God. God's wisdom shines brighter than any kind of human understanding. It is only fitting that we should give Him all of the accolades and keep none for ourselves.

To help in our search for wisdom, we can and should ask for prayers from people whom we recognize as being gifted with godly wisdom. Throughout the Bible, we see how wise leaders have bequeathed wisdom to selected others. For example, Moses laid hands on Joshua: *"Now Joshua the son of Nun was filled with the spirit of wisdom, for Moses had laid his hands on him; and the sons of Israel listened to him and did as the* Lord *had commanded Moses"* (Deuteronomy 34:9).

Don't forget the value of praying in the Spirit. Paul wrote, *"I will pray with the spirit and I will pray with the mind also; I will sing with the spirit and I will sing with the mind also"* (1 Corinthians 14:15). By praying with our spirits and praying in the Holy Spirit (in an unknown tongue that is furnished by the Spirit), we can move far beyond our natural understanding. The gift of tongues is not the least of the gifts of the Spirit, as many people assume. I always call it the "entrance ramp" into all of the other gifts. Praying and singing in the Spirit is transrational in nature, bypassing our cerebral understanding as we tap into the mind of Christ.

When you pray in the Spirit, you enter the realm of spiritual gifts; next, you might find the gift of faith rising up, or a word of wisdom, or a word of knowledge, or discerning of spirits, or whatever else the Spirit of God knows that you need at that moment. Jude sums it up this way in his letter: *"But you, dear friends, must build up your lives ever more strongly upon the foundation of our holy faith, learning to pray in the power and strength of the Holy Spirit"* (Jude 1:20 TLB).

The Word of God itself supplies much wisdom. As you read your Bible day after day and year after year, new levels of revelation and understanding will unfold in your mind and heart. The Word of God is *alive* with divine life. The psalmist wrote about it, *"The unfolding of your words gives light; it gives understanding to the simple"* (Psalm 119:130 NIV). This effect is completely unique to the Word of God; no amount of human education or natural intelligence can match it.

When you read (or sing or hear) God's Word, the Spirit sheds light on your decisions, even the small ones. In a way that you cannot ascertain or describe, the Word imparts wisdom to you, along with knowledge and correction and a host of other blessings. *"For the word of God is alive and active. Sharper than any double-edged sword, it penetrates even to dividing soul and spirit, joints and marrow; it judges the thoughts and attitudes of the heart"* (Hebrews 4:12 NIV). God's Word gives you the wisdom to know what to do with your insights and feelings.

Solomon described the way he approached it like this: *"I set my mind to seek and explore by wisdom concerning all that has been done under heaven"* (Ecclesiastes 1:13). He set his mind to gain all the wisdom that he could. The *New King James Version* translates it as *"I set my heart...."* The word *"heart"* may speak better to Feelers than the word *"mind."* In any case, we need to apply ourselves to seeking wisdom, and we need to explore in many directions as we search.

> **AS YOU READ YOUR BIBLE DAY AFTER DAY AND YEAR AFTER YEAR, NEW LEVELS OF REVELATION AND UNDERSTANDING WILL UNFOLD IN YOUR MIND AND HEART.**

In my own life, I needed to gain wisdom and understanding about the Feeler realm, about my own sensitivity, and about the sensitivity of others. I spent years searching the Scriptures on the subject. I even read a top-level secular book that greatly helped me along my own path of exploration. I did more research. I prayed a lot. I had a dream or two. I started to put the pieces together. I sat with other gifted people. I journaled about my encounters. I waited and worshipped and prayed some more.

Throughout this process, I kept my mind and heart set on the goal of gaining wisdom and understanding about highly sensitive people, who I am now referring to as Feelers, so they can be effective followers of Christ and empowered ministers for God. This book is the result—and I pray that you are gaining wisdom and insight from this integrated approach.

DEMONSTRATING WISDOM

If you go looking through the Bible for evidence of God's gift of wisdom in action, you may be surprised at the range of examples you will find. Wisdom is important!

Of course, we think of Solomon first. God answered his prayer abundantly:

> *God said to Solomon, "Since this is your heart's desire and you have not asked for wealth, possessions or honor, nor for the death of your enemies, and since you have not asked for a long life but for wisdom and knowledge to govern my people over whom I have made you king, therefore wisdom and knowledge will be given you. And I will also give you wealth, possessions and honor, such as no king who was before you ever had and none after you will have."*
>
> (2 Chronicles 1:11–12 NIV)

Solomon committed plenty of errors in his life, some of them major; nevertheless, he was known for his abundant wisdom. It can be an encouragement to us all to know that our mistakes and faulty decisions do not disqualify us from operating in the wisdom of God; perhaps, they should only increase our sense of need for more wisdom.

Then there is Daniel. When Daniel was challenged to interpret King Nebuchadnezzar's dream without even being given the benefit of learning what the dream was about, he sought God's wisdom. God gave him such astounding knowledge and insight that he could actually tell the king what the dream contained, as well as what it meant. Daniel praised God, saying, *"I thank and praise you, God of my ancestors: you have given me wisdom and power, you have made known to me what we asked of you, you have made known to us the dream of the king"* (Daniel 2:23 NIV).

Part of the wisdom of God is to value the insights He gives, not brushing them off lightly or forgetting them. Mary, the mother of Jesus, when she was still a young teenager, had been visited by the angel Gabriel, conceived the Messiah through the overshadowing of the Holy

Spirit, given birth to the Son of God, and been visited by shepherds who'd heard the news of her Son's arrival by a host of heavenly angels. What did she do? She treasured in her heart all of these supernatural encounters. She pondered what they could mean; she plumbed the depths of her faith-filled understanding so that she could cooperate with God as fully as possible:

> But she was very perplexed at this [Gabriel's] statement, and kept pondering what kind of salutation this was.　　　　(Luke 1:29)

> Mary treasured up all these things and pondered them in her heart.　　　　　　　　　　　　　　　　(Luke 2:19 NIV)

And then, of course, when her Son, Jesus, began to mature, one of the aspects of His maturity was increased wisdom: *"Jesus kept increasing in wisdom and stature, and in favor with God and men"* (Luke 2:52). We too, must mature in wisdom.

Such examples provide us with a picture of what we are aiming for. Even though none of us will ever be another Solomon or Daniel or Mary or Jesus, we can exemplify God's wisdom through our words and actions just the same. As a commodity, wisdom is a jewel of a gift, but, sadly, it is rarely on display in the body of Christ.

For Feelers in particular, it is important to seek God's wisdom and use it in our everyday living. We tend to become overly serious and self-focused, thinking everything is all about us. We may pick up on someone else's problem and think it is our own because we lack the discernment and wisdom to know what to do with the information. We can become very "me centered" and do way too much "navel gazing."

Some of us Feelers need to dial it down, avoid letting our emotions consume us, and flat-out get a life! Get out of the house; go on a drive. Take up a new hobby. Learn to love the great outdoors. Exercise. Yes, you heard me. Too many introverted Feelers use their temperament as an excuse to be couch potatoes. Feelers are often really good at being devotional "Mary's," but it would do us some good to go "feed the poor" and be a "Martha" every now and then. Get out of your comfort zone. Build community. Connect! Grow!

Again, like Jesus did when He was on earth, we need to grow in wisdom and stature and favor.

WISDOM INSIGHTS FOR FEELERS

Wisdom comes by experience, communion with the Lord, and dialogue with others. A key to true growth and spiritual maturity is asking the right questions of the right people with the right motivation.

As you assess what you are sensing, you must also learn to ask yourself questions all the time. What are some examples of the right kind of questions to ask yourself? Early on, as you begin to sense something, you need to gain specific wisdom regarding your next steps, and you can ask yourself questions such as the following:

- What (or who) is the source of these feelings?
- Are these God's emotions, or are they mine only?
- Am I picking up emotions from people around me?
- Could these feelings be coming from an evil regional principality?
- Are these feelings being sanctified and filtered properly?
- Have I stayed grounded in the Word of God?
- What does the Word say about this?
- Am I rooted in a healthy community of believers?
- With whom should I share this sense before I do something with it? Who can give me sound advice?
- Do I know someone who exemplifies wisdom? Can I learn something new from that person? Could I ask that person to pray for me to have wisdom?
- Am I discerning external atmospheres?

+ How should I respond to this sense? Have I prayed for the Lord to give me wisdom about it?

+ Is this feeling something I'm supposed to address, or should I simply note and acknowledge it without taking action?

+ Am I supposed to pray about what I'm sensing and not take any outward action?

The answer to the question "How should I respond?" will depend not only on the situation but also on your gift-based kingdom calling. If God has called you to be an intercessor, you may find that praying is the wisest course of action to take with most of the things you sense. You may need to pray persistently, carrying a burden for a period of time. But you may not need to pray more than once, because some matters require only a onetime prayer. You may need to enlist the prayer assistance of other intercessors, or you may not—it all depends on what God tells you to do. Too many intercessors get caught up in unsanctified emotions, carrying a matter far beyond their allotment of grace.[42] Don't be one of them! Use wisdom!

WISDOM COMES BY EXPERIENCE, COMMUNION WITH THE LORD, AND DIALOGUE WITH OTHERS.

If God has called you to be a prophet in the body of Christ, you probably already know something about determining when and how and to whom to release a word. Mostly through trial and error, you will have already acquired a lot of wisdom about that. The larger community of Feeler-prophets can provide you with additional insights about timing, modes of expression, biblical boundaries, and safeguards.

---

42. For more information on this topic, see my book *Praying with God's Heart*.

Many Feelers will not have an identifiable avenue of expression, such as intercession or prophecy, for the senses they pick up. For any of us, basic wisdom includes the biblical advice to be *"quick to listen, slow to speak"* (James 1:19 NIV, NLT). In other words, pay attention to what you are sensing, and listen to the Holy Spirit. Then, listen some more. Do not act with haste.

TAKING BABY STEPS

We don't judge a baby's innate abilities at the moment of their birth or when the child takes their first few wobbly steps. Similarly, we must recognize that, as a Feeler "child" is learning to operate in the Feeler realm, they will totter and fall often, only to get up again to take more steps. As a Feeler, commit yourself to seeking wisdom first for your own life, the lives of your family members, and the lives of the people in your sphere of responsibility. As you do so, you will obtain wisdom regarding the greater integration of the Feeler realm into your everyday life.

There is safety in the community of believers. Don't isolate yourself, even if you sometimes feel rejected. No one can claim to be wise if they are separated from the body of Christ. We are better together, and only together! Even God lives in community! Have you ever thought of that?

It is crucial to have a yielded life. Find your security and identity in Christ Jesus—not in any of your gifts, callings, functions, or unique expressions of sensitivity. Your function in life will change from one season to the next. If you are finding your security in a position, then that is a sure setup for an eventual crash. Our only sure foundation is found in Jesus Christ, and in Him alone. He is the rock of our salvation!

And, if you need some healing in overcoming the rejection syndrome, Jesus is great at providing that as well. Jesus came to heal the brokenhearted and to set the captives free. (See Isaiah 61:1.) Jesus is the Great Physician, and *"whosoever shall call on the name of the LORD shall be delivered"* (Joel 2:32 KJV)!

You are a disciple of Jesus Christ and a child of the Father, with the Holy Spirit dwelling inside you. What a joy it is to know that God made you the way you are—and that He will bring you to maturity and fruit-fulness. And so, there you have a little bit of wisdom for Feelers that I have picked up along the way.

PRAYER OF A PASSIONATE HEART

Gracious Father, I magnify the name of Your Son, Jesus Christ. I declare that I want to grow in wisdom and stature and favor, just as He did. I honor the pioneers who have gone before me and am grateful for what their lives can teach me. I pray to exemplify the three-cord strand of the fullness of character, fullness of power, and fullness of God's wisdom, and I ask You to bring these aspects together in my life. Please lead me, teach me, and guide me. Equip me with the wisdom I need to serve You freely. I love You because You first loved me. Amen.

12

Flowing in the Power of God

"Anyone who believes in me may come and drink! For the Scriptures declare, 'Rivers of living water will flow from his heart.'"
—John 7:38 (NLT)

Interestingly, survival experts apply the "rule of threes" to living without the essentials of life, including air, shelter, water, and food. Humans can go about three minutes without air, three hours without shelter in a harsh environment, three days without water, and three weeks without food.

Focusing on our need for water, Jesus tells His disciples that if we believe in Him, *"rivers of living water"* will flow out from within us, from our hearts.

Rivers are a source of life. Entire civilizations have been built along waterways because of the access to flowing water for drinking, bathing, and transporting both goods and people far and wide. Rivers wash the landscape and help supply the oceans to overflowing.

As it is in the natural, so it is in the spiritual. Again, Jesus declared that *rivers* of living water would flow from within anyone who believes in Him, and most believers are familiar with at least some level of that supernatural flow. This is because His followers serve as temples for the indwelling Holy Spirit, and the rivers that flow from our innermost beings were prefigured in the swiftly rising river that flowed from the temple in Ezekiel's vision:

> The man brought me back to the entrance to the temple, and **I saw water coming out from under the threshold of the temple** toward the east (for the temple faced east). The water was coming down from under the south side of the temple, south of the altar. He then brought me out through the north gate and led me around the outside to the outer gate facing east, and **the water was trickling** from the south side. As the man went eastward with a measuring line in his hand, he measured off a thousand cubits and then led me through **water that was ankle-deep.** He measured off another thousand cubits and led me through **water that was knee-deep.** He measured off another thousand and led me through **water that was up to the waist.** He measured off another thousand, but now it was a river that I could not cross, because **the water had risen and was deep enough to swim in—a river that no one could cross.**
>
> (Ezekiel 47:1–5 NIV)

In subsequent verses, we read that everywhere the water went, there was life. (See Ezekiel 47:7–12.) In fact, because of the unending supply of water, great and fruitful trees could grow up on both banks of the river. This tells us something about the essential flow of the life-giving rivers that spring from within us—if they are not blocked in any way.

At first, after we test the water of the river of life, we learn to wade in it, and then we learn to swim in it, even if it seems to take us places we never expected to go.

RIVERS CONVERGING

In the opening of my book *The Seer,* I wrote about the Nile River, the longest river in the world, and how it is formed when two other rivers flow together into it: the White Nile and the Blue Nile. I saw it as analogous for the way the stream of the prophet and the stream of the seer combine to make a mighty prophetic river. It's similar to the way the Missouri River and the Ohio River, among others, combine to form the mighty Mississippi River in the United States.

In terms of the flow of the river of living water, I propose that a third stream is also converging with the others—the stream of the Feeler. When you add the life-giving stream of the Feeler realm to the prophetic and visionary realms, you get a very mighty river indeed! Greater convergence means greater power and impact.

Three other expressions of rivers of God are also combined to form the flow of our ministry in the power of the Holy Spirit: (1) ministering in *faith*, (2) ministering by *the gifts of the Spirit*, and (3) ministering by *the realm of glory*. Each of these expressions can be held up to the light and considered in terms of how it relates to the Feeler realm.

> **WHEN YOU ADD THE LIFE-GIVING STREAM OF THE FEELER REALM TO THE PROPHETIC AND VISIONARY REALMS, YOU GET A VERY MIGHTY RIVER INDEED!**

MINISTERING IN FAITH

Faith is always important, and everything else depends upon it. That's what the writer of Hebrews tells us: *"You can never please God without faith, without depending on him. Anyone who wants to come to God must believe that there is a God and that he rewards those who sincerely look for him"* (Hebrews 11:6 TLB). We must live by faith every day. *"Jesus said, 'Did I not tell you that if you believe, you will see the glory of God?'"* (John 11:40 NIV).

When you are already filtering everything through your faith, you can see more clearly. You can more calmly face whatever challenges come your way, and you are content to be a humble servant of the One in whom you have placed your faith. Paul wrote to the Roman believers, *"For by the grace given me I say to every one of you: Do not think of yourself more highly than you ought, but rather think of yourself with sober judgment, in accordance with the faith God has distributed to each of you"* (Romans 12:3 NIV).[43]

Obviously, we must minister by faith. In fact, we must follow the lead of our faith, even when our senses have not indicated any particular course of action. Feelers need to recognize this reality when confronted with situations where they can't feel out what to do. Is somebody sick? Just pray for that person, even if you don't feel any heat in your hands or you forgot to bring anointing oil. *"And the prayer offered in faith will restore the one who is sick, and the Lord will raise him up"* (James 5:15). Your faith is more consistent than your feelings are—even your Holy Spirit-anointed feelings.

Remember that you don't need a special gift of faith every time you minister in Jesus's name. Even small faith—if it is flowing with the new life Jesus pours into you—is adequate: *"Truly I say to you, if you have faith the size of a mustard seed, you will say to this mountain, 'Move from here to there,' and it will move; and nothing will be impossible to you"* (Matthew 17:20).

MINISTERING BY THE GIFTS OF THE SPIRIT

By faith, we minister with both the supernatural and the natural gifts that God has supplied, going wherever the Spirit "blows" us:

> *Since we have gifts that differ according to the grace given to us, each of us is to exercise them accordingly: if prophecy, according to the proportion of his faith; if service, in his serving; or he who teaches, in his teaching; or he who exhorts, in his exhortation; he who gives,*

---

43. For more about the gift and the fruit of faith, see my book *Radical Faith*.

with liberality; he who leads, with diligence; he who shows mercy, with cheerfulness.   (Romans 12:6–8)

As already explained, every believer has God-imparted gifts with which to minister:

There are different kinds of gifts, but the same Spirit distributes them. There are different kinds of service, but the same Lord. There are different kinds of working, but in all of them and in everyone it is the same God at work. Now to each one the manifestation of the Spirit is given for the common good. To one there is given through the Spirit a message of wisdom, to another a message of knowledge by means of the same Spirit, to another faith by the same Spirit, to another gifts of healing by that one Spirit, to another miraculous powers, to another prophecy, to another distinguishing between spirits, to another speaking in different kinds of tongues, and to still another the interpretation of tongues. All these are the work of one and the same Spirit, and he distributes them to each one, just as he determines.
(1 Corinthians 12:4–11 NIV)

The question we have been exploring and deciphering in this book is this: "How does ministry work when you bring in the Feeler realm?" Our faith, our gifts, and even the glory of God are greatly enhanced when we liberate all of our senses with the help of the Helper. The gifts of the Holy Spirit are now working in tandem with our surrendered, healed, and empowered five natural senses, and we are transformed into supernatural change agents!

MINISTERING BY THE REALM OF GLORY

You may consider yourself an ordinary Christian who has never experienced what it is like to minister to others in Jesus's name while standing in the manifest presence of God, or what many of us refer to as the "glory realm." Open heavens are a part of revival culture in both the Old and the New Testament and a part of both our Jewish and church history. There are geographical places and times where it seems that the veil between heaven and earth is much more permeable.

My friend Joshua Mills, a purehearted lover of Jesus, has written a book called *Power Portals* that discusses these very things.[44] One of Joshua's mentors, the late Ruth Ward Heflin, author of *Harvest Glory*, was a forerunner of ministering in the glory realm. Long before these believers, there was a woman evangelist named Maria Woodworth-Etter, born in 1844, who ministered in the glory. If you want to stretch your faith and learn about ministering in the power of God, then consider reading her work *Signs and Wonders*.[45] The list goes on and on.

> **OPEN HEAVENS ARE A PART OF REVIVAL CULTURE IN BOTH THE OLD AND THE NEW TESTAMENT AND A PART OF BOTH OUR JEWISH AND CHURCH HISTORY.**

Please don't rule this out for your life. Just as that fire-starter Randy Clark has stated, "God can use little ole me!" Just keep zealously seeking His presence, and the day may come when the sheer presence of the living God in your life is enough to work miracles, and you will rejoice with these words of Isaiah:

> *Arise, shine; for your light has come, and the glory of the LORD has risen upon you. For behold, darkness will cover the earth and deep darkness the peoples; but the LORD will rise upon you and His glory will appear upon you.*   (Isaiah 60:1–2)

---

44. Joshua Mills, *Power Portals* (New Kensington, PA: Whitaker House, 2020).
45. Maria Woodworth-Etter, *Signs and Wonders* (New Kensington, PA: Whitaker House, 1997).

MINISTERING OUT OF YOUR KNOWER

Now let's really go after another interrelated subject. The Feeler and the Knower are deeply connected and can be connectors to moving in the power of God.

Did you know that you have more than one center from which your knower operates? Right now, let's call each of these centers a "brain." That's right—you actually have three centers where these revelatory, knower realms work. The Holy Spirit uses each one of these command centers to communicate to us and within us in a unique way.

I became exposed to this understanding from a son in the faith of mine, Matt Sorger. We were ministering together at a prophetic conference in Minnesota along with one of my mentors, Mahesh Chavda. So, we had a true "joining of the generations" present. Stacey Campbell, a renowned ecstatic prophetess who is also a dear friend and fellow pioneer, was a part of the prophetic panel that afternoon as well.

A question from the moderator was sent in Matt's direction concerning how he perceived revelation from the Holy Spirit. He responded by sharing the concept of "the three brains." My spiritual antennae went way out, and I thought, "Now, that is one of the missing pieces! I really need to capture and incorporate this!"

Matt said that he'd come across the idea of our having three brains from viewing a science program. He was especially interested in it because, when he was in university, he studied several sciences, including biology, in preparation for going into the field of medicine. It was in the midst of his studies that God called him to preach the Word of God, so he let go of his pursuit of being a medical doctor.

At the conference, Matt went on to talk more about this idea, and I will summarize his points in the paragraphs that follow.

First is the "head brain." This is the brain we refer to when talking about the brain in general. The head brain consists of brain cells called neurons, and it functions mostly through logical thought, but it is also involved in subconscious thought and in our dream life.

One of the other two centers of knowledge, or command centers, is the "heart brain." (I will describe the third command center below.) The human heart contains 40,000 neurons, nerve cells that have the capacity to store memory.

After the conference, Matt continued to share this concept with me. There was a documented case of a young girl who needed a heart transplant. After she received her new heart, she began to have dreams in which she saw herself being killed and could see the face of her murderer. This information was eventually given to the police. As it turned out, her heart donor was a murder victim. The police made a sketch of the face of the man in her dreams, and that person was caught and brought to justice.

The knowledge stored in the heart brain can be so useful for the ministry of inner healing and deliverance. When we talk about healing past traumas and memories, we don't just ask God to heal the memories in our "head brain"; we also need to pray over the stored memories and emotions in our "heart brain."

This has a lot to do with the realm of feelings, doesn't it? Some additional divine pieces of the puzzle seem to be coming together. But wait, there is more!

The third command center of communications is the "gut brain." Each of us has a third brain, per se, in our gut. The entire lining of our intestines is filled with neurons—over 100 million of them!

If you have ever used the phrase "I had a gut feeling," you may have been on to something! The neurons in your gut have the ability to process knowledge on an intuitive level. Your head brain processes logical knowledge; your gut brain processes intuitive knowledge and can literally know something in advance of your head brain.

This is why it may take your head some time to catch up to your gut. And this is why Feelers, in particular, will say things like, "I just don't feel right about it in my gut," or, on the flip side, "I know this is it! I have a really good feeling about this. Yes, my gut feeling says move forward and act fast while the window is still open!"

FEELING WHAT JESUS FEELS

Whatever form your ministry takes, you must press in to know God better so that you can feel what Jesus feels and follow through on what His Spirit wants you to do.

I touched on this topic previously, but one of the main feelings you can be looking for is a surge of compassion. When you are confronted with someone's need, are you "moved with compassion" for the other person, as Jesus was? *"Moved with compassion, Jesus reached out and touched him. 'I am willing,' he said. 'Be healed!'"* (Mark 1:41 NLT). When you feel a surge of loving compassion, you can know that He is near and that your prayers will be more effective.

> **WHATEVER FORM YOUR MINISTRY TAKES, YOU MUST PRESS IN TO KNOW GOD BETTER SO THAT YOU CAN FEEL WHAT JESUS FEELS AND FOLLOW THROUGH ON WHAT HIS SPIRIT WANTS YOU TO DO.**

Jesus could even feel it when His compassionate healing power was drawn out of Him. I'm thinking of the account of the woman with the hemorrhage who crept up to be near Him in the crowd, hoping she would not be noticed, because her condition made her unclean by the standards of the Jewish laws. Perhaps you remember the story:

Now a certain woman had a flow of blood for twelve years, and had suffered many things from many physicians. She had spent all that she had and was no better, but rather grew worse. When she heard about Jesus, she came behind Him in the crowd and touched His garment. For she said, "If only I may touch His clothes, I shall be made well." Immediately the fountain of her blood was dried up, and she felt in her body that she was healed of the affliction. And Jesus, immediately knowing in Himself that power had gone out of Him, turned around in the crowd and said, "Who touched My clothes?" But His disciples said to Him, "You see the multitude thronging You, and You say, 'Who touched Me?'" And He looked around to see her who had done this thing. But the woman, fearing and trembling, knowing what had happened to her, came and fell down before Him and told Him the whole truth. And He said to her, "Daughter, your faith has made you well. Go in peace, and be healed of your affliction." (Mark 5:25–34 NKJV)

The woman had touched only Jesus's clothing, yet He felt power go out of Himself. The King James version of the Bible calls this power *"virtue."* Jesus had neither heard nor seen her, and in the jostling crowd, her touch could not have been perceived, and yet He had felt the release of the living river inside Him. *"Who touched My clothes?"* He said, turning.

The woman was terrified, not only because she had been shunned as unclean for so many years and had hoped to touch Jesus's hem without being noticed, but also because she could tell by the way her body felt that her impossible medical condition had been instantly healed. However, she did not need to be afraid. The Lord told her in a quiet voice, *"Daughter, your faith has made you well. Go in peace, and be healed of your affliction."*

People who are desperate for a touch of God can draw the anointing forth. It can happen with you and with me. And we may feel God's compassion along with it.

Jesus told a parable in which forgiveness was released through compassion. It is known as the parable of the unforgiving servant or the parable of the unmerciful servant. (See Matthew 18:21–35.) The servant was deeply in debt, and the ruler to whom he owned the money threatened to throw him and his family into debtor's prison. But when the servant begged for mercy, *"the master of that servant was moved with compassion, released him, and forgave him the debt"* (Matthew 18:27 NKJV). The rest of the parable shows how, in direct contrast to the mercy he had just been shown, the servant tried to force a fellow servant to repay a small debt he owed him. Although he had just been forgiven for a massive debt, he lacked the compassion of the ruler. There is value in paying attention to a feeling of godly compassion, which may signal the release of forgiveness just as much as it does the release of physical healing or the like.

Incidentally, speaking of feelings and forgiveness, remember that when you need to forgive someone, you may not feel like doing it at all. To forgive is an act of a person's will, and it is difficult. Your feelings may run more along the lines of hurt and outrage, which may make you able to recognize yourself in one of the scriptural passages about forgiveness. I think of the one that comes right before the parable of the unforgiving servant, when Peter asked Jesus how many times a person is required to forgive the sin of another: "'...*Up to seven times?' Jesus said to him, 'I do not say to you, up to seven times, but up to seventy times seven'*" (Matthew 18:21–22). You must simply do the right thing and forgive from your heart, ignoring your conflicted feelings. In due time, your feelings will catch up, and you will feel free to love again.

RIVERS OF LIVING WATER

Jesus was led by the Spirit to do what the Father was doing. He was grounded in the Word of God. And He was sensitive to the flow of the anointing coming upon Him and through Him. What is the anointing? It is God's power released to accomplish His supernatural purposes. It can manifest like a feeling, a surge of authority, or a presence of calm and peace that comes upon you. Every believer can and should learn how to flow with the Spirit in their everyday life.

You and I can learn to pay closer attention to the divine flow upon and through our own lives, and using emotional language can help us understand what God is doing. Most of the time, we will not be praying over someone for healing; we will be just going through our ordinary routines. During those long stretches of "just living," we can and should be able to stay in close touch with the Holy Spirit. We can keep moving in the river of God's presence, for example, by noticing our fruit-of-the-Spirit feelings—love, joy, peace, patience, kindness, gentleness, goodness, faithfulness, and self-control. Pay attention to how you are feeling during the day, even when your feelings are subtle, and express your delight to the Lord.

You may find yourself saying:

+ "I feel so loved! Now I know a little better what it means to be the beloved of the Lord."

+ "I can't stop laughing! The joy of the Lord is my strength." (See Nehemiah 8:10.)

+ "I can't think of anything except _____. It's like a weight on my soul. Help me with it, Lord."

+ "That heavy burden has lifted at last, and I can sense the peace and grace of God."

+ "Oh, look at that beautiful _____! I'm so grateful for the beauty around me, Lord."

+ "My heart feels lighter and my whole being feels refreshed. Being in the presence of God is wonderful."

+ "That music brings tears of joy to my eyes."

+ "Father, I can feel Your comforting hand on my shoulder, and now I know I'm Your child. You help me every day."

+ "I can feel quiet strength coming into my soul. Now I know I'll make it through this long trial."

When the Holy Spirit is directing you to reach out to others in service or ministry, you may sense His guidance in various ways. You may feel pain or heat in a specific part of your body when the Lord is present to heal someone through your prayers. When He wants you to step into a leadership role, you may feel something like the weight of a mantle settling on your shoulders, or you may feel something touch your forehead.

As mentioned earlier in the chapter, you may feel the compassion of the Lord toward someone and, with it, an inspiration to meet that person's need in the power and grace of God. You may sense the presence of supernatural faith in someone and identify it so that the person can release it for its intended purpose. You may see, either with your natural eyes or with the eyes of your spirit, angels or other manifestations of the Lord's presence.

At times, a person may simply cross your mind. If you are paying attention, you will know whether God wants you to reach out to the person in some way at that moment, and whether He wants you to stop what you're doing and pray for the person. You could pick up on just about anything with your senses, and God will always supply the "interpretation" so you know what to do. It is my hope and prayer that this book has equipped you to operate in the Feeler realm with integrity and joy.

WORD AND SPIRIT TOGETHER

Too often, we in the body of Christ have suffered a divorce between the two very necessary, complementary aspects of the kingdom of God—the Word of God and the Spirit of God, represented by evangelical Christians and Pentecostal/charismatic Christians. To move into the greater works of Jesus, we need a marriage between these two aspects, not a divorce. We need to return to the Acts 13 model in which the school of the Word and the school of the Spirit cooperated together. (See Acts 13:1–2.)

> *WE NEED TO RETURN TO THE ACTS 13 MODEL IN WHICH THE SCHOOL OF THE WORD AND THE SCHOOL OF THE SPIRIT COOPERATED TOGETHER.*

By combining our gifts in the grace of God, we can step into the greater-works generation with those who have taken to heart Jesus's words in John 14:12: *"I tell you the truth, anyone who believes in me will do the same works I have done, and even greater works, because I am going to be with the Father"* (NLT).

If we work together, God's power can flow freely and revive the dry places on the face of the earth. Let's drink deeply and allow His refreshing river to spill out!

> *Ho! Every one who thirsts, come to the waters; and you who have no money come, buy and eat. Come, buy wine and milk without money and without cost.... And the LORD will continually guide you, and satisfy your desire in scorched places, and give strength to your bones; and you will be like a watered garden, and like a spring of water whose waters do not fail.*   (Isaiah 55:1; 58:11)

Let's rejoice! The Seers have role models and instructions on how to see as Jesus sees. The Hearers have many mentors and equipping tools to help them hear God for themselves. We are grateful that quality teaching has come forth to help us each grow in our discernment in these days. And, finally, the highly sensitive Feelers also have emerging role models coming together in the Word and the Spirit. Praise the Lord, it is a new day, and there are fresh understandings for a new era!

PRAYER OF A PASSIONATE HEART

Father, I am amazed at Your ways, and I purpose to unite myself with Your people as You lead me. I am grateful for all of the streams and tributaries that are joining together into a mighty river of life in this day. I pray to know and flow in that river of Your presence and power. I give all the glory to You. Send Your Spirit more powerfully, for Jesus Christ's sake, as I offer thanksgiving and praise in His mighty name. Again I say, amen!

Additional Resources by James W. Goll

(Many titles feature a matching study guide, as well as audio and video presentations.)

Adventures in the Prophetic (with Michal Ann Goll, Mickey Robinson, Patricia King, Jeff Jansen, and Ryan Wyatt)

Angelic Encounters (with Michal Ann Goll)

The Call to the Elijah Revolution (with Lou Engle)

Deliverance from Darkness

The Discerner

Dream Language (with Michal Ann Goll)

Exploring Your Dreams and Visions

Finding Hope

God Encounters Today (with Michal Ann Goll)

Hearing God's Voice Today

The Lifestyle of a Prophet

The Lifestyle of a Watchman

The Lost Art of Intercession

The Lost Art of Practicing His Presence

The Lost Art of Pure Worship (with Chris Dupré and contributions from Jeff Deyo, Sean Feucht, Julie Meyer, and Rachel Goll Tucker)

Living a Supernatural Life

The Mystery of Israel and the Middle East

Passionate Pursuit

Prayer Storm

The Prophet

The Prophetic Intercessor

A Radical Faith

Releasing Spiritual Gifts Today

The Scribe

The Seer

Shifting Shadows of Supernatural Experiences (with Julia Loren)

Women on the Frontlines series: *A Call to Compassion, A Call to Courage,* and *A Call to the Secret Place* (Michal Ann Goll with James W. Goll)

About the Author

James W. Goll is the founder of God Encounters Ministries. He is an international bestselling author, a certified Life Language Coach, an adviser to leaders and ministries, and a recording artist. He is also the founder of Worship City Alliance and Prayer Storm, and the cofounder of Compassion Acts and Women on the Frontlines. James is a member of the Harvest International Ministries International Apostolic Team and the Apostolic Council of Prophetic Elders. He serves as a core instructor in the Wagner University. James is also the founder of GOLL Ideation LLC, where creativity, consulting, and leadership training come together.

After pastoring in the Midwest United States, James was thrust into the role of an international equipper and trainer. He has traveled to over fifty nations, sharing the love of Jesus and imparting the power of intercession, prophetic ministry, and life in the Spirit. His desire is to see the body of Christ become the house of prayer for all nations and to see Jesus Christ receive the rewards for His sufferings.

James has recorded numerous classes with corresponding curriculum kits, and he also offers a yearlong mentoring program available globally at mentoringwithjames.com. He is the author of more than fifty books, including *The Seer*, *The Discerner*, *Strike the Mark*, *Releasing Spiritual Gifts Today*, *Dream Language*, *Praying with God's Heart*, and *The Mystery of Israel and the Middle East*.

James was married to Michal Ann for thirty-two years before her graduation to heaven in the fall of 2008. He has four married children and a growing number of grandchildren. He makes his home in Franklin, Tennessee.

For more information:

James W. Goll

God Encounters Ministries

P.O. Box 1653
Franklin, TN 37065
Phone: 1-877-200-1604

Websites:

godencounters.com
mentoringwithjames.com/GEM
GOLLIdeation.com

E-mails:

info@godencounters.com
linktr.ee/GodEncounters

Social Media:

Facebook, Instagram, Twitter, Parlor, YouTube, Vimeo, GEM Media, XP Media, Kingdom Flame, Charisma blogs, iTunes podcasts